Exploring Data

Counting Ourselves and Others

Kindergarten
Also appropriate for Grade 1

Karen Economopoulos
Susan Jo Russell

Developed at TERC, Cambridge, Massachusetts

Dale Seymour Publications®
White Plains, New York

Some material in this unit was developed by Susan Jo Russell and Antonia Stone for *Counting: Ourselves and Our Families* (a unit in the series *Used Numbers: Real Data in the Classroom*), ©1990 by Dale Seymour Publications®.

The *Investigations* curriculum was developed at TERC (formerly Technical Education Research Centers) in collaboration with Kent State University and the State University of New York at Buffalo. The work was supported in part by National Science Foundation Grant No. ESI-9050210. TERC is a nonprofit company working to improve mathematics and science education. TERC is located at 2067 Massachusetts Avenue, Cambridge, MA 02140.

This project was supported, in part, by the
National Science Foundation
Opinions expressed are those of the authors
and not necessarily those of the Foundation

Managing Editor: Catherine Anderson
Series Editor: Beverly Cory
Manuscript Editor: Nancy Tune
ESL Consultant: Nancy Sokol Green
Production/Manufacturing Director: Janet Yearian
Production/Manufacturing Manager: Karen Edmonds
Production/Manufacturing Coordinator: Roxanne Knoll
Design Manager: Jeff Kelly
Design: Don Taka
Composition: Joe Conte
Illustrations: DJ Simison
Cover: Bay Graphics

This book is published by Dale Seymour Publications®, an imprint of Addison Wesley Longman, Inc.

Dale Seymour Publications
10 Bank Street
White Plains, NY 10602
Customer Service: 1-800-872-1100

Order number DS47107
ISBN 1-57232-930-0
8 9 10-ML-03 02

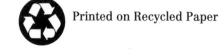

Printed on Recycled Paper

INVESTIGATIONS IN NUMBER, DATA, AND SPACE®

T E R C

Principal Investigator Susan Jo Russell

Co-Principal Investigator Cornelia Tierney

Director of Research and Evaluation Jan Mokros

Director of K–2 Curriculum Karen Economopoulos

Curriculum Development

Karen Economopoulos
Rebeka Eston
Marlene Kliman
Christopher Mainhart
Jan Mokros
Megan Murray
Kim O'Neil
Susan Jo Russell
Tracey Wright

Evaluation and Assessment

Mary Berle-Carman
Jan Mokros
Andee Rubin

Teacher Support

Irene Baker
Megan Murray
Kim O'Neil
Judy Storeygard
Tracey Wright

Technology Development

Michael T. Battista
Douglas H. Clements
Julie Sarama

Video Production

David A. Smith
Judy Storeygard

Administration and Production

Irene Baker
Amy Catlin

**Cooperating Classrooms
for This Unit**

Jeanne Wall
*Arlington Public Schools
Arlington, MA*

Audrey Barzey
Patricia Kelliher
Ellen Tait
*Boston Public Schools
Boston, MA*

Meg Bruton
*Fayerweather Street School
Cambridge, MA*

Rebeka Eston
*Lincoln Public Schools
Lincoln, MA*

Lila Austin
*The Atrium School
Watertown, MA*

Christopher Mainhart
*Westwood Public Schools
Westwood, MA*

Consultants and Advisors

Deborah Lowenberg Ball
Michael T. Battista
Marilyn Burns
Douglas H. Clements
Ann Grady

CONTENTS

WHERE TO START

The first-time user of *Counting Ourselves and Others* should read the following:

When you next teach this same unit, you can begin to read more of the background. Each time you present the unit, you will learn more about how your students understand the mathematical ideas.

Investigations in Number, Data, and Space® is a K–5 mathematics curriculum with four major goals:

- to offer students meaningful mathematical problems
- to emphasize depth in mathematical thinking rather than superficial exposure to a series of fragmented topics
- to communicate mathematics content and pedagogy to teachers
- to substantially expand the pool of mathematically literate students

The *Investigations* curriculum embodies a new approach based on years of research about how children learn mathematics. Each grade level consists of a set of separate units, each offering 2–8 weeks of work. These units of study are presented through investigations that involve students in the exploration of major mathematical ideas.

Approaching the mathematics content through investigations helps students develop flexibility and confidence in approaching problems, fluency in using mathematical skills and tools to solve problems, and proficiency in evaluating their solutions. Students also build a repertoire of ways to communicate about their mathematical thinking, while their enjoyment and appreciation of mathematics grows.

The investigations are carefully designed to invite all students into mathematics—girls and boys, members of diverse cultural, ethnic, and language groups, and students with different strengths and interests. Problem contexts often call on students to share experiences from their family, culture, or community. The curriculum eliminates barriers—such as work in isolation from peers, or emphasis on speed and memorization—that exclude some students from participating successfully in mathematics. The following aspects of the curriculum ensure that all students are included in significant mathematics learning:

- Students spend time exploring problems in depth.
- They find more than one solution to many of the problems they work on.

- They invent their own strategies and approaches, rather than rely on memorized procedures.
- They choose from a variety of concrete materials and appropriate technology, including calculators, as a natural part of their everyday mathematical work.
- They express their mathematical thinking through drawing, writing, and talking.
- They work in a variety of groupings—as a whole class, individually, in pairs, and in small groups.
- They move around the classroom as they explore the mathematics in their environment and talk with their peers.

While reading and other language activities are typically given a great deal of time and emphasis in elementary classrooms, mathematics often does not get the time it needs. If students are to experience mathematics in depth, they must have enough time to become engaged in real mathematical problems. We believe that a minimum of 5 hours of mathematics classroom time a week—about an hour a day—is critical at the elementary level. The scope and pacing of the *Investigations* curriculum are based on that belief.

We explain more about the pedagogy and principles that underlie these investigations in Teacher Notes throughout the units. For correlations of the curriculum to the NCTM Standards and further help in using this research-based program for teaching mathematics, see the following books, available from Dale Seymour Publications:

- *Implementing the* Investigations in Number, Data, and Space® *Curriculum*
- *Beyond Arithmetic: Changing Mathematics in the Elementary Classroom* by Jan Mokros, Susan Jo Russell, and Karen Economopoulos

This book is one of the curriculum units for *Investigations in Number, Data, and Space*. In addition to providing part of a complete mathematics curriculum for your students, this unit offers information to support your own professional development. You, the teacher, are the person who will make this curriculum come alive in the classroom; the book for each unit is your main support system.

Although the curriculum does not include student instructional texts, reproducible sheets for student work are provided with the units and, in some cases, are also available as Student Activity Booklets. In these investigations, students work actively with objects and experiences in their own environment, including manipulative materials and technology, rather than with a workbook.

Ultimately, every teacher will use these investigations in ways that make sense for his or her particular style, the particular group of students, and the constraints and supports of a particular school environment. Each unit offers information and guidance drawn from our collaborations with many teachers and students over many years. Our goal is

to help you, a professional educator, give all your students access to mathematical power.

Investigation Format

The opening two pages of each investigation help you get ready for the work that follows.

- **Focus Time** This gives a synopsis of the activities used to introduce the important mathematical ideas for the investigation.
- **Choice Time** This lists the activities, new and recurring, that support the Focus Time work.
- **Mathematical Emphasis** This highlights the most important ideas and processes students will encounter in this investigation.
- **Teacher Support** This indicates the Teacher Notes and Dialogue Boxes included to help you understand what's going on mathematically in your classroom.
- **What to Plan Ahead of Time** These lists alert you to materials to gather, sheets to duplicate, and other things you need to do before starting the investigation. Full details of materials and preparation are included with each activity.

INVESTIGATION 1

How Many Are We?

Focus Time

How Many Are We? (p. 4)
In this investigation, students make several different representations of their class—the group of people for whom they will be collecting data over the entire unit. They begin by counting the people in the class and making individual recordings of their results.

Counting Noses, Counting Eyes (p. 16)
Students suggest ways of counting noses in the classroom. They take the count and make a representation of the result. Then they list body parts that come in twos and finish by making a class "eye chart."

Choice Time

Self-Portraits (p. 25)
Students create detailed self-portraits, which they sort into groups according to attributes such as hair color or types of clothing.

Counting Chairs (p. 28)
Students count chairs to determine whether there are enough for everyone in the class. They make a representation to show their work.

Pattern Block Grab (p. 30)
Students grab a handful of pattern blocks and then make a representation that shows how many and what kinds of blocks they grabbed.

Mathematical Emphasis

- Developing and using strategies for counting
- Relating counting to the quantity of items in a group
- Using one-to-one correspondence
- Exploring two-to-one correspondence
- Recording and representing data in a variety of ways
- Looking at different representations of the same data set
- Sorting objects into groups by attribute

Teacher Support

Teacher Notes
From the Classroom: How Many Are We? (p. 10)
Counting Is More Than 1, 2, 3 (p. 12)
Inventing Pictures of the Data (p. 13)
One-to-One Correspondence (p. 14)
Dealing with Sensitive Issues (p. 33)
Two-to-One Correspondence (p. 34)

Dialogue Boxes
Why Do We Need to Know? (p. 9)
Counting Eyes (p. 35)

INVESTIGATION 1

What to Plan Ahead of Time

Focus Time Materials

How Many Are We?
- Cubes, buttons, counters
- Art materials such as dot stickers, 1-inch squares of colored paper, crayons, markers, colored pencils, glue sticks
- Large drawing paper (at least 11 by 17 inches): 1 sheet per student

Counting Noses, Counting Eyes
- Interlocking cubes: 2 per student plus extras
- Index cards, 3 by 5 inches: 1 per student
- Crayons or markers
- Chart, 8 inches by about 6 feet (length varies with class size)
- Chart paper: 3 sheets
- Small mirrors to share (optional)
- Glue sticks or tape

Choice Time Materials

Self-Portraits
- Drawing paper (at least 6 by 9 inches): 1 per student plus extras
- Crayons or other drawing materials
- Small mirrors to share (optional)

Counting Chairs
- Clipboards: 1 per student (optional); can be made by attaching a sheet of paper to a book or stiff cardboard with a large paper clip, clothespin, or binder clip
- Unlined paper: 1 per student plus extras
- Counters: a large supply
- Art supplies

Pattern Block Grab
- Pattern blocks: 1 bucket per 4–6 students
- Unlined paper: 1 sheet per student
- Crayons or markers

Family Connection
- Family letter (p. 110): 1 per family, or *Investigations* at Home
- Counting Eyes at Home (p. 111): 1 per student, for optional homework

Preparation for Investigation 2
- Start collecting containers such as small boxes, empty plastic bottles, and canned goods for use in Investigation 2. To solicit help from families, duplicate and send home Help Stock Our Class Store (p. 112).

Always read through an entire investigation before you begin, in order to understand the overall flow and sequence of the activities.

Focus Time In this whole-group meeting, you introduce one or more activities that embody the important mathematical ideas underlying the investigation. The group then may break up into individuals or pairs for further work on the same activity. Many Focus Time activities culminate with a brief sharing time or discussion as a way of acknowledging students' work and highlighting the mathematical ideas. Focus Time varies in length. Sometimes it is short and can be completed in a single group meeting or a single work period; other times it may stretch over two or three sessions.

Choice Time Each Focus Time is followed by Choice Time, which offers a series of supporting activities to be done simultaneously by individuals, pairs, or small groups. You introduce these related tasks over a period of several days. During Choice Time, students work independently, at their own pace, choosing the activities they prefer and often returning many times to their favorites. Many kindergarten classrooms have an activity time built into their daily schedule, and Choice Time activities can easily be incorporated.

Together, the Focus Time and Choice Time activities offer a balanced kindergarten curriculum.

Classroom Routines The kindergarten day is filled with opportunities to work with mathematics. Routines such as taking attendance, asking about snack preferences, and discussing the calendar offer regular, ongoing practice in counting, collecting and organizing data, and understanding time.

Four specific routines—Attendance, Counting Jar, Calendar, and Today's Question—are formally introduced in the unit *Mathematical Thinking in Kindergarten*. Another routine, Patterns on the Pocket Chart, is introduced in the unit *Pattern Trains and Hopscotch Paths*. Descriptions of these routines can also be found in an appendix for each unit, and reminders of their ongoing use appear in the Unit Overview charts.

The Linguistically Diverse Classroom Each unit includes an appendix with Tips for the Linguistically Diverse Classroom to help teachers support stu-

dents at varying levels of English proficiency. While more specific tips appear within the units at grades 1–5, often in relation to written work, general tips on oral discussions and observing the students are more appropriate for kindergarten.

Also included are suggestions for vocabulary work to help ensure that students' linguistic difficulties do not interfere with their comprehension of math concepts. The Preview for the Linguistically Diverse Classroom lists key words in the unit that are generally known to English-speaking kindergartners. Activities to help familiarize other students with these words are found in the appendix, Vocabulary Support for Second-Language Learners. In addition, ideas for making connections to students' languages and cultures, included on the Preview page, help the class explore the unit's concepts from a multicultural perspective.

Materials

A complete list of the materials needed for teaching this unit follows the Unit Overview. These materials are available in *Investigations* kits or can be purchased from school supply dealers.

Classroom Materials In an active kindergarten mathematics classroom, certain basic materials should be available at all times, including interlocking cubes, a variety of things to count with, writing and drawing materials. Some activities in this curriculum require scissors and glue sticks or tape; dot stickers and large paper are also useful. So that students can independently get what they need at any time, they should know where the materials are kept, how they are stored, and how they are to be returned to the storage area.

Children's Literature Each unit offers a list of children's literature that can be used to support the mathematical ideas in the unit. Sometimes an activity incorporates a specific children's book, with suggestions for substitutions where practical. While such activities can be adapted and taught without the book, the literature offers a rich introduction and should be used whenever possible. If you can get the titles in Big Book format, these are ideal for kindergarten.

Blackline Masters Student recording sheets and other teaching tools for both class and homework are provided as reproducible blackline masters at the end of each unit. When student sheets are designated for kindergarten homework, they usually repeat an activity from class, such as playing a game, as a way of involving and informing family members. Occasionally a homework sheet may ask students to collect data or materials for a class project or in preparation for upcoming activities.

Student Activity Booklets For the two kindergarten number units, the blackline masters are also available as Student Activity Booklets, designed to free you from extensive copying. The other kindergarten units require minimal copying.

Family Letter A letter that you can send home to students' families is included with the blackline masters for each unit. Families need to be informed about the mathematics work in your classroom; they should be encouraged to participate in and support their children's work. A reminder to send home the letter for each unit appears in one of the early investigations. These letters are also available separately in Spanish, Vietnamese, Cantonese, Hmong, and Cambodian.

***Investigations* at Home** To further involve families in the kindergarten program, you can offer them the *Investigations* at Home booklet, which describes the kindergarten units, explains the mathematics work children do in kindergarten, and offers activities families can do with their children at home.

Adapting *Investigations* to Your Classroom

Kindergarten programs vary greatly in the amount of time each day that students attend. We recommend that kindergarten teachers devote from 30 to 45 minutes daily to work in mathematics, but we recognize that this can be challenging in a half-day program. The kindergarten level of *Investigations* is intentionally flexible so that teachers can adapt the curriculum to their particular setup.

Kindergartens participating in the *Investigations* field test included full-day programs, half-day programs of approximately 3 hours, and half-day programs that add one or two full days to the kindergarten week at some point in the school year. Despite the wide range of program structures, classrooms generally fell into one of two groups: those that offered a separate math time daily (Math Workshop or Math Time), and those that included one or two mathematics activities during a general Activity Time or Station Time.

Math Workshop Teachers using a Math Workshop approach set aside 30 to 45 minutes each day for doing mathematics. In addition, they usually also have a more general activity time in their daily schedule. On some days, Math Workshop might be devoted to the Focus Time activities, with the whole class gathered together. On other days, students might work in small groups and choose from three or four Choice Time activities.

Math as Part of Activity Time Teachers with less time in their day may offer students one or two math activities, along with activities from other areas of the curriculum, during their Activity Time or Station Time. For example, on a particular day, students might be able to choose among a science activity, block building, an art project, dramatic play, books, puzzles, and a math activity. New activities are introduced during a whole-class meeting. With the *Investigations* curriculum, teachers who use this approach have found that it is important to designate at least one longer block of time (30 to 45 minutes) each week for mathematics. During this time, students engage in Focus Time activities and have a chance to share their work and discuss mathematical ideas. The suggested Choice Time activities are then presented as part of the general activity time. Following this model, work on a curriculum unit will naturally stretch over a longer period.

Planning Your Curriculum The amount of time scheduled for mathematics work will determine how much of the kindergarten *Investigations* curriculum a teacher is able to cover in the school year. You may have to make some choices as you adapt the units to your particular schedule. What is most important is finding a way to involve students in mathematics every day of the school year.

Each unit will be handled somewhat differently by every teacher. You need to be active in determining an appropriate pace and the best transition points for your class. As you read an investigation, make some preliminary decisions about how many days you will need to present the activities, based on what you know about your students and about your schedule. You may need to modify your initial plans as you proceed, and you may want to make notes in the margins of the pages as reminders for the next time you use the unit.

Help for You, the Teacher

Because we believe strongly that a new curriculum must help teachers think in new ways about mathematics and about their students' mathematical thinking processes, we have included a great deal of material to help you learn more about both.

About the Mathematics in This Unit This introductory section summarizes the essential information about the mathematics you will be teaching. It describes the unit's central mathematical ideas and the ways students will encounter them through the unit's activities.

Teacher Notes These reference notes provide practical information about the mathematics you are teaching and about our experience with how students learn. Many of the notes were written in response to actual questions from teachers or to discuss important things we saw happening in the field-test classrooms. Some teachers like to read them all before starting the unit, then review them as they come up in particular investigations.

In the kindergarten units, Teacher Notes headed "From the Classroom" contain anecdotal reflections of teachers. Some focus on classroom management issues, while others are observations of students at work. These notes offer another perspective on how an activity might unfold or how kindergarten students might become engaged with a particular material or activity.

A few Teacher Notes touch on fundamental principles of using *Investigations* and focus on the pedagogy of the kindergarten classroom:

- About Choice Time
- Materials as Tools for Learning
- Encouraging Students to Think, Reason, and Share Ideas
- Games: The Importance of Playing More Than Once

After their initial appearance, these are repeated in the back of each unit. Reviewing these notes periodically can help you reflect on important aspects of the *Investigations* curriculum.

Dialogue Boxes Sample dialogues demonstrate how students typically express their mathematical ideas, what issues and confusions arise in their thinking, and how some teachers have guided class discussions.

Many of these dialogues are word-for-word transcriptions of recorded class discussions. They are not always easy reading; sometimes it may take some effort to unravel what the students are trying to say. But this is the value of these dialogues; they offer good clues to how your students may develop and express their approaches and strategies, helping you prepare for your own class discussions.

Where to Start You may not have time to read everything the first time you use this unit. As a first-time user, you will likely focus on understanding the activities and working them out with your students. You will also want to read the few sections listed in the Contents under the heading Where to Start.

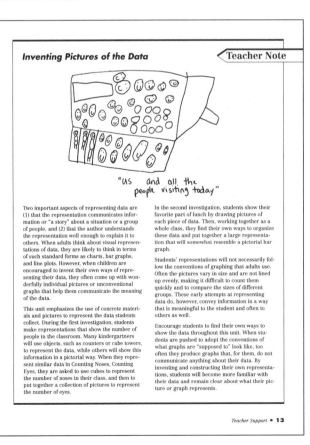

Inventing Pictures of the Data ⟨Teacher Note⟩

"us and all the people visiting today"

Two important aspects of representing data are (1) that the representation communicates information or "a story" about a situation or a group of people, and (2) that the author understands the representation well enough to explain it to others. When adults think about visual representations of data, they are likely to think in terms of such standard forms as charts, bar graphs, and line plots. However, when children are encouraged to invent their own ways of representing their data, they often come up with wonderfully individual pictures or unconventional graphs that help them communicate the meaning of the data.

This unit emphasizes the use of concrete materials and pictures to represent the data students collect. During the first investigation, students make representations that show the number of people in the classroom. Many kindergartners will use objects, such as counters or cube towers, to represent the data, while others will show this information in a pictorial way. When they represent similar data in Counting Noses, Counting Eyes, they are asked to use cubes to represent the number of noses in their class, and then to put together a collection of pictures to represent the number of eyes.

In the second investigation, students show their favorite part of lunch by drawing pictures of each piece of data. Then, working together as a whole class, they find their own ways to organize these data and put together a large representation that will somewhat resemble a pictorial bar graph.

Students' representations will not necessarily follow the conventions of graphing that adults use. Often the pictures vary in size and are not lined up evenly, making it difficult to count them quickly and to compare the sizes of different groups. These early attempts at representing data do, however, convey information in a way that is meaningful to the student and often to others as well.

Encourage students to find their own ways to show the data throughout this unit. When students are pushed to adopt the conventions of what graphs are "supposed to" look like, too often they produce graphs that, for them, do not communicate anything about their data. By inventing and constructing their own representations, students will become more familiar with their data and remain clear about what their picture or graph represents.

Teacher Support ■ 13

The *Investigations* curriculum incorporates the use of two forms of technology in the classroom: calculators and computers. Calculators are assumed to be standard classroom materials, available for student use in any unit. Computers are explicitly linked to one or more units at each grade level; they are used with the unit on 2-D geometry at each grade, as well as with some of the units on measuring, data, and changes.

Using Calculators

In this curriculum, calculators are considered tools for doing mathematics, similar to pattern blocks or interlocking cubes. Just as with other tools, students must learn both *how* to use calculators correctly and *when* they are appropriate to use. This knowledge is crucial for daily life, as calculators are now a standard way of handling numerical operations, both at work and at home. Calculators are formally introduced in the grade 1 curriculum, but if available, can be introduced to kindergartners informally.

Using a calculator correctly is not a simple task; it depends on a good knowledge of the four operations and of the number system, so that students can select suitable calculations and also determine what a reasonable result would be. These skills are the basis of any work with numbers, whether or not a calculator is involved.

Unfortunately, calculators are often seen as tools to check computations with, as if other methods are somehow more fallible. Students need to understand that any computational method can be used to check any other; it's just as easy to make a mistake on the calculator as it is to make a mistake on paper or with mental arithmetic. Throughout this curriculum, we encourage students to solve computation problems in more than one way in order to double-check their accuracy. We present mental arithmetic, paper-and-pencil computation, and calculators as three possible approaches.

In this curriculum we also recognize that, despite their importance, calculators are not always appropriate in mathematics instruction. Like any tools, calculators are useful for some tasks but not for others. You will need to make decisions about when to allow students access to calculators and when to ask that they solve problems without them, so that they can concentrate on other tools and skills. At times when calculators are or are not appropriate for a particular activity, we make specific recommendations. Help your students develop their own sense of which problems they can tackle with their own reasoning and which ones might be better solved with a combination of their own reasoning and the calculator.

Managing calculators in your classroom so that they are a tool, and not a distraction, requires some planning. When calculators are first introduced, students often want to use them for everything, even problems that can be solved quite simply by other methods. However, once the novelty wears off, students are just as interested in developing their own strategies, especially when these strategies are emphasized and valued in the classroom. Over time, students will come to recognize the ease and value of solving problems mentally, with paper and pencil, or with manipulatives, while also understanding the power of the calculator to facilitate work with larger numbers.

Experience shows that if calculators are available only occasionally, students become excited and distracted when permitted to use them. They focus on the tool rather than on the mathematics. In order to learn when calculators are appropriate and when they are not, students must have easy access to them and use them routinely in their work.

If you have a calculator for each student, and if you think your students can accept the responsibility, you might allow them to keep their calculators with the rest of their individual materials, at least for the first few weeks of school. Alternatively, you might store them in boxes on a shelf, number each calculator, and assign a corresponding number to each student. This system can give students a sense of ownership while also helping you keep track of the calculators.

Using Computers

Students can use computers to approach and visualize mathematical situations in new ways. The computer allows students to construct and manipulate geometric shapes, see objects move according to rules they specify, and turn, flip, and repeat a pattern.

This curriculum calls for computers in units where they are a particularly effective tool for learning mathematics content. One unit on 2-D geometry at each of the grades 3–5 includes a core of activities that rely on access to computers, either in the classroom or in a lab. Other units on geometry, measurement, data, and changes include computer activities, but can be taught without them. In these units, however, students' experience is greatly enhanced by computer use.

The following list outlines the recommended use of computers in this curriculum:

Kindergarten
Unit: *Making Shapes and Building Blocks*
   (Exploring Geometry)
Software: *Shapes*
Source: Provided with the unit

Grade 1
Unit: *Survey Questions and Secret Rules*
   (Collecting and Sorting Data)
Software: *Tabletop, Jr.*
Source: Broderbund

Unit: *Quilt Squares and Block Towns*
   (2-D and 3-D Geometry)
Software: *Shapes*
Source: provided with the unit

Grade 2
Unit: *Mathematical Thinking at Grade 2*
   (Introduction)
Software: *Shapes*
Source: provided with the unit

Unit: *Shapes, Halves, and Symmetry*
   (Geometry and Fractions)
Software: *Shapes*
Source: provided with the unit

Unit: *How Long? How Far?* (Measuring)
Software: *Geo-Logo*
Source: provided with the unit

Grade 3
Unit: *Flips, Turns, and Area* (2-D Geometry)
Software: *Tumbling Tetrominoes*
Source: provided with the unit

Unit: *Turtle Paths* (2-D Geometry)
Software: *Geo-Logo*
Source: provided with the unit

Grade 4
Unit: *Sunken Ships and Grid Patterns*
   (2-D Geometry)
Software: *Geo-Logo*
Source: provided with the unit

Grade 5
Unit: *Picturing Polygons* (2-D Geometry)
Software: *Geo-Logo*
Source: provided with the unit

Unit: *Patterns of Change* (Tables and Graphs)
Software: *Trips*
Source: provided with the unit

Unit: *Data: Kids, Cats, and Ads* (Statistics)
Software: *Tabletop, Sr.*
Source: Broderbund

The software provided with the *Investigations* units uses the power of the computer to help students explore mathematical ideas and relationships that cannot be explored in the same way with physical materials. With the *Shapes* (grades K–2) and *Tumbling Tetrominoes* (grade 3) software, students explore symmetry, pattern, rotation and reflection, area, and characteristics of 2-D shapes. With the *Geo-Logo* software (grades 2–5), students investigate rotations and reflections, coordinate geometry, the properties of 2-D shapes, and angles. The *Trips* software (grade 5) is a mathematical exploration of motion in which students run experiments and interpret data presented in graphs and tables.

We suggest that students work in pairs on the computer; this not only maximizes computer resources but also encourages students to consult, monitor, and teach one another. However, asking more than two students to work at the same computer is less effective. Managing access to computers is an issue for every classroom. The curriculum gives you explicit support for setting up a system. The units are structured on the assumption that you have enough computers for half your students to work on the machines in pairs at one time. If you do not have access to that many computers, suggestions are made for structuring class time to use the unit with fewer than five.

Assessment plays a critical role in teaching and learning, and it is an integral part of the *Investigations* curriculum. For a teacher using these units, assessment is an ongoing process. You observe students' discussions and explanations of their ideas and strategies on a daily basis and examine their work as it evolves. While students are busy working with materials, playing mathematical games, sharing ideas with partners, and working on projects, you have many opportunities to observe their mathematical thinking. What you learn through observation guides your decisions about how to proceed, both with the curriculum and with individual students.

Our experiences with young children suggest that they know, can explain, and can demonstrate with materials a lot more than they can represent on paper. This is one reason why it is so important to engage children in conversation, helping them explain their thinking about a problem they are solving. It is also why, in kindergarten, assessment is based exclusively on a teacher's observations of students as they work.

The way you observe students will vary throughout the year. At times you may be interested in particular strategies that students are developing to solve problems. Other times, you might want to observe how students use or do not use materials for solving problems. You may want to focus on how students interact when working in pairs or groups. You may be interested in noting the strategy that a student uses when playing a game during Choice Time. Or you may take note of student ideas and thinking during class discussions.

Assessment Tools in the Unit

Virtually every activity in the kindergarten units of the *Investigations* curriculum includes a section called Observing the Students. This section is a teacher's primary assessment tool. It offers guidelines on what to look for as students encounter the mathematics of the activity. It may suggest questions you can ask to uncover student thinking or to stimulate further investigation. When useful, a range of potential responses or examples of typical student approaches are given, along with ways to adapt the activity for students in need of more or less challenge.

Supplementing this main assessment tool in each unit are the Teacher Notes and Dialogue Boxes that contain examples of student work, teacher observations, and student conversations from real kindergarten classrooms. These resources can help you interpret experiences from your own classroom as you progress through a unit.

Documentation of Student Growth

You will probably need to develop some sort of system to record and keep track of your observations. A single observation is like a snapshot of a student's experience with a particular activity, but when considered over time, a collection of these snapshots provides an informative and detailed picture of a student. Such observations are useful in documenting and assessing student's growth, as well as in planning curriculum.

Observation Notes A few ideas that teachers have found successful for record keeping are suggested here. The most important consideration is finding a system that really works for you. All too often, keeping observation notes on a class of 20–30 students is overwhelming and time-consuming. Your goal is to find a system that is neither.

Some teachers find that a class list of names is convenient for jotting down their observations. Since the space is limited, it is not possible to write lengthy notes; however, over time, these short observations provide important information.

Other teachers keep a card file or a loose-leaf notebook with a page for each student. When something about a student's thinking strikes them as important, they jot down brief notes and the date.

Some teachers use self-sticking address labels, kept on clipboards around the classroom. After taking notes on individual students, they simply peel off each label and stick it into the appropriate student file or notebook page.

You may find that writing notes at the end of each week works well for you. For some teachers, this process helps them reflect on individual students, on the curriculum, and on the class as a whole. Planning for the next weeks' activities often grows out of these weekly reflections.

Student Portfolios Collecting samples of student work from each unit in a portfolio is another way to document a student's experience that supports your observation notes. In kindergarten, samples of student work may include constructions, patterns, or designs that students have recorded, score sheets from games they have played, and early attempts to record their problem-solving strategies on paper, using pictures, numbers, or words.

The ability to record and represent one's ideas and strategies on paper develops over time. Not all 5- and 6-year-olds will be ready for this. Even when students are ready, what they record will have meaning for them only in the moment—as they work on the activity and make their representation. You can augment this by taking dictation of a student's idea or strategy. This not only helps both you and the student recall the idea, but also gives students a model of how their ideas could be recorded on paper.

Over the school year, student work samples combined with anecdotal observations are valuable resources when you are preparing for family conferences or writing student reports. They help you communicate student growth and progress, both to families and to the students' subsequent teachers.

Assessment Overview

There are two places to turn for a preview of the assessment information in each kindergarten *Investigations* unit. The Assessment Resources column in the Unit Overview chart locates the Observing the Students section for each activity, plus any Teacher Notes and Dialogue Boxes that explain what to look for and what types of responses you might see in your classroom. Additionally, the section called About the Assessment in This Unit gives you a detailed list of questions, keyed to the mathematical emphases for each investigation, to help you observe and assess student growth. This section also includes suggestions for choosing student work to save from the unit.

These examples illustrate record keeping systems used by two different teachers for the kindergarten unit *Collecting, Counting, and Measuring,* one using the class list and the other using individual note cards to record student progress.

Emma Ruiz

3/19 Counting Jar: counts 9 balls accurately and makes another set of 9 cubes

3/24 Today's Question: compares data, "13 is 4 more than 9 because the 13 tower is 4 names taller."

4/1 Draws counting Book pictures for 1-6, then adds pgs 7, 8, 9, 10, 11 on her own

Unit: *Collecting, Counting, and Measuring*
Activity: *Inventory Bags*
Date: 10/12 and 10/13

Alexa • counting sequence to 50↑ • counts 1:1 up to 12 • counts 4 bags accurately	Luke • counts to 30, misses 19, 20 and 29, 30 • counts by moving objects; 1:1 to 10 objects • draws circles for buttons
Ayesha • works with Oscar • counts to 15 accurately – trouble beyond 15 but Oscar helps ★ Meet to check • 1:1 to 8 objects? counting	Maddy • difficult to tell how much M. counted herself + how much was done by partner. Work w/ her to see.
Brendan absent 10/12, 10/13	Miyuki • counts aloud beyond 30 but leaves out 14 • counts 1:1 up to 10 but doesn't organize objects
Carlo • counts objects with difficulty. • remove items from bag so he works with 10 • says numbers to 10, counts objects to 6	Oscar • works with Ayesha • counts rotely to 20, maybe higher • double-checks his count every time – is accurate
Charlotte • completed inventory task easily without help • counts accurately up to 20 objects • represents with numbers	Ravi • worked w/ his aide to complete task • counts 1:1 to 5 objects • difficulty representing quantity w/ pictures
Felipe • worked well with Tarik • counted ~ — 21 in all	Renata

Counting Ourselves and Others

Content of This Unit Throughout this unit, students count to collect information about themselves, their classmates, and their environment. They also begin to sort objects, such as pattern blocks, types of containers, and items of clothing, and to sort and classify data: What are our favorite lunch foods? What are some different ways to categorize those foods? Along with counting and categorizing data, students work to represent their results with physical models or on paper. Students later conduct their own surveys within the class, making decisions about the questions they will ask and how they will keep track of the information they gather. They complete the process by studying the results to see what their survey showed. In the final investigation, students solve a mathematical problem based on the day's attendance data.

Connections with Other Units If you are doing the full-year *Investigations* curriculum in the suggested sequence for kindergarten, this is the fourth of six units. The work in this unit is an extension of the data activities introduced in *Mathematical Thinking in Kindergarten*. It complements and supports work with counting presented in the units *Collecting, Counting, and Measuring* and *How Many in All?*

The unit can also be used successfully at grade 1, depending on the needs and previous experience of your students.

Investigations Curriculum ■ Suggested Kindergarten Sequence

Mathematical Thinking in Kindergarten (Introduction)

Pattern Trains and Hopscotch Paths (Exploring Pattern)

Collecting, Counting, and Measuring (Developing Number Sense)

▶ *Counting Ourselves and Others* (Exploring Data)

Making Shapes and Building Blocks (Exploring Geometry)

How Many in All? (Counting and the Number System)

Investigation 1 ▪ How Many Are We?

Class Sessions	Activities	Pacing
FOCUS TIME (p. 4) How Many Are We?	Counting the Class Representing the Count Sharing Representations	1–2 sessions
FOCUS TIME (p. 16) Counting Noses, Counting Eyes	How Many Noses? How Many Eyes? Making a Class "Eye Chart" Homework: Eyes at Home	1–2 sessions
CHOICE TIME (p. 25)	Self-Portraits Counting Chairs Pattern Block Grab	3–4 sessions
Classroom Routines	Attendance and Calendar (daily) Counting Jar, Today's Question, and Patterns on the Pocket Chart (weekly or as appropriate)	

Mathematical Emphasis

- Developing and using strategies for counting

- Relating counting to the quantity of items in a group

- Using one-to-one correspondence

- Exploring two-to-one correspondence

- Representing data in a variety of ways

- Looking at different representations of the same data set

- Sorting objects into groups by attribute

Assessment Resources

Observing the Students:

- Representing the Count (p. 7)

- How Many Noses? (p. 18)

- Making a Class "Eye Chart" (p. 22)

- Self-Portraits (p. 27)

- Counting Chairs (p. 29)

- Pattern Block Grab (p. 31)

Teacher Note: How Many Are We? (p. 10)

Teacher Note: Counting Is More Than 1, 2, 3 (p. 12)

Teacher Note: One-to-One Correspondence (p. 14)

Teacher Note: Two-to-One Correspondence (p. 34)

Materials

Interlocking cubes

Counters such as buttons

Dot stickers, colored paper squares

Crayons, markers, colored pencils

Glue sticks

Large drawing paper

Mirrors (optional)

Index cards (3 by 5 inches)

Clipboards (optional)

Pattern blocks

Unlined paper

Chart paper

Teaching resource sheets

Interlocking cubes

Investigation 2 ▪ What Did You Eat for Lunch?

Class Sessions	Activities	Pacing
FOCUS TIME (p. 38) What Did You Eat for Lunch?	Favorite Lunch Foods Sorting the Lunch Foods Extension: Shoe Data	1–2 sessions
CHOICE TIME (p. 44)	Same and Different Boxes, Bottles, and Cans The Grocery Store Clothing Sort	4–5 sessions
Classroom Routines	Attendance and Calendar (daily) Counting Jar, Today's Question, and Patterns on the Pocket Chart (weekly or as appropriate)	

Mathematical Emphasis

- Collecting, recording, and representing data

- Organizing a set of data in more than one way

- Noting similarities and differences in related objects

- Sorting by attribute into two groups

- Sorting a set of objects in more than one way

- Discussing the information in a data representation

Assessment Resources

Observing the Students:

- Same and Different (p. 45)

- Boxes, Bottles, and Cans (p. 47)

- The Grocery Store (p. 49)

- Clothing Sort (p. 52)

Teacher Note: Choosing Categories (p. 53)

Teacher Note: Questions That Promote Data Analysis (p. 54)

Dialogue Box: But My Peach Was Sweet (p. 55)

Materials

This Is the Way We Eat Our Lunch by Edith Baer (optional)

Index cards (5 by 8 inches)

Crayons or markers

Glue sticks

Unlined paper

Butcher paper

Chart paper

Pairs of objects for sorting

Small boxes, plastic bottles, and cans for sorting

Storage boxes

Empty grocery containers

Sets of clothing in three distinct sizes

Student Sheet 1

Assorted boxes, bottles, and cans

Investigation 3 ▪ Collecting Data About Our Class

Class Sessions	Activities	Pacing
FOCUS TIME (p. 58) Yes/No Surveys	Are You Here Today? Choosing Survey Questions Collecting Survey Data	1–2 sessions
CHOICE TIME (p. 66)	Yes/No Surveys Boxes, Bottles, and Cans The Grocery Store Pattern Block Grab	4–5 sessions
Classroom Routines	Attendance and Calendar (daily) Counting Jar, Today's Question, and Patterns on the Pocket Chart (weekly or as appropriate)	

Mathematical Emphasis

- Composing survey questions
- Gathering and recording survey data
- Comparing the sizes of different groups in a survey
- Making sense of data representations
- Sorting by attribute into two groups
- Describing categories for a sort

Assessment Resources

Observing the Students:

- Collecting Survey Data (p. 64)
- Yes/No Surveys (p. 67)

Teacher Note: Examining Young Students' Data Representations (p. 69)

Dialogue Box: Are You Here Today? (p. 72)

Materials

Clothespins

Survey board (cardboard or poster board)

Class lists

Unlined paper

Clipboards (optional)

Small boxes, plastic bottles, and cans for sorting

Empty grocery containers

Pattern blocks

Crayons or markers

Chart paper

Student Sheet 2

Pattern blocks

Investigation 4 ▪ Who's Here? Who's Not?

Class Sessions	Activities	Pacing
FOCUS TIME (p. 78) Who's Here? Who's Not?	How Many Are Here Today? How We Solved the Problem Extension: Counting Strategies	1 session
CHOICE TIME (p. 81)	Yes/No Surveys The Grocery Store	2–3 sessions
Classroom Routines	Attendance and Calendar (daily) Counting Jar, Today's Question, and Patterns on the Pocket Chart (weekly or as appropriate)	

Mathematical Emphasis

- Solving a mathematical problem based on data

- Building a model or making a representation to explain a problem-solving strategy

- Counting and comparing sets of objects or people

Assessment Resources

Observing the Students:

- How Many Are Here Today? (p. 80)

Teacher Note: How Many Are Here Today? (p. 82)

Teacher Note: Understanding Students' Work (p. 84)

Materials

Counters (buttons, cubes)

Dot stickers, colored paper squares

Crayons, markers, colored pencils

Glue sticks

Drawing paper

Unlined paper

Clipboards (optional)

Empty grocery containers

Art materials

Following are the basic materials needed for the activities in this unit. Many items can be purchased from the publisher, either individually or in the Teacher Resource Package and the Student Materials Kit for kindergarten. Detailed information is available on the *Investigations* order form. To obtain this form, call toll-free 1-800-872-1100 and ask for a Dale Seymour customer service representative.

Snap™ Cubes (interlocking cubes): class set, or 1 tub per 4–6 students

Pattern blocks: 1 bucket per 4–6 students

Counters (buttons, cubes): a large supply

Small mirrors (optional)

Clipboards, or make from sturdy cardboard and binder clips (optional)

This Is the Way We Eat Our Lunch by Edith Baer (optional)

Spring-clip clothespins: 1 per student

Boxes, bottles, and unopened cans for sorting (may be brought from home): at least 8–10 of each kind of container,

Empty grocery item containers (may be brought from home) for class store

Items of clothing (e.g., shirt, pants, socks, shoes, gloves/mittens, hat, coat/sweater) in three distinct sizes: infant or toddler, kindergarten-age, and adult

Dot stickers, colored paper, glue sticks, tape

Crayons, markers, colored pencils

Unlined paper

Chart paper

Index cards, 3 by 5 inches and 5 by 8 inches: one of each size per student, plus extras

Large drawing paper (11 by 17 inches or larger)

Butcher paper

Poster board or cardboard: single sheet, 8 by 36 inches

Storage boxes

The following materials are provided at the end of this unit as blackline masters.

Family Letter (p. 110)

Student Sheets 1–2 (p. 113)

Teaching Resources

    Counting Eyes at Home (p. 111)

    Help Stock Our Class Store (p. 112)

    Choice Board Art (p. 115)

Related Children's Literature

Baer, Edith. *This Is the Way We Eat Our Lunch.* New York: Scholastic, 1995.

Baer, Edith. *This Is the Way We Go to School.* New York: Scholastic, 1990.

Lobel, Arnold. "The Lost Button," in *Frog and Toad Are Friends.* New York: HarperCollins, 1970.

Reid, Margarette. *The Button Box.* New York: Dutton Children's Books, 1990.

Winthrop, Elizabeth. *Shoes.* Harper & Row, 1986.

Collecting, representing, and interpreting information are ongoing activities in our daily lives. In today's world, these activities are vital to our ability to understand events and make decisions. Young students' natural curiosity makes them avid collectors of materials and information. Working with data builds on their desire to know about their world and the people in it. In this unit students count, sort, classify, and represent information—each process an important part of data analysis and of the kindergarten mathematics curriculum.

Through the activities in this unit, students explore three important aspects of data: (1) data can be collected by counting; (2) data can be sorted and classified according to common attributes, and (3) data can be represented through pictures, graphs, and models.

Counting in Data Collection Counting is an important way for children to develop an understanding of what numbers mean. Students may start kindergarten thinking of counting as a string of words, but they make a gradual transition to using counting as a tool for describing their world. In order to count successfully, students must remember the rote counting sequence, assign one counting number to each object counted, and at the same time have a strategy for keeping track of what has already been counted and what still needs to be counted. As students practice counting, and as they listen to and watch others count, they will develop successful and meaningful counting strategies.

When students collect data, they are counting in very real ways. Central to any data collection activity is the need to establish the group of people or objects being considered. Knowing how many are in that group encourages students to develop strategies for keeping track of who has been counted. It also reinforces the one-to-one correspondence between the number of people in the group and the total number of responses collected and represented.

Sorting and Classifying Data Identifying and describing attributes of an object are essential in defining that object. By using attributes to see how things are the same and different, we are able to sort things into groups and classify them by those attributes. Sorting and classifying are useful tools in all areas of mathematics. For example, being able to describe the attributes of a square and think about how it is the same as and different

Sorting and classifying data about ourselves

"Brown Hair"

from other four-sided figures helps create a definition of a square.

Sorting and classifying are central to organizing and interpreting data. As students think about how pieces of information are the same and different, they begin to form the basis for determining how data might be grouped and how those groups might be defined. While kindergarten students are not yet ready to consider many attributes at the same time, they are excellent observers; they often think about how things go together in an effort to make sense out of their world. Throughout the unit, students gain experience in describing, sorting, and defining the information they collect, and they begin to develop categorization skills by making decisions about what categories to use and which data belong in which categories.

Representing Data Our world is flooded with examples of different types of graphs, charts, and other visual organizations of data, all intended to communicate specific information. Students need to look at and understand different kinds of representations so that they can make sense out of the information presented and become critical readers of data.

Kindergarten students communicate a great deal of information about what they know and think through their drawings and through concrete models. In this unit, as students collect and use data to solve mathematical problems, they build models and make representations on paper that communicate their results and their problem-solving strategies to others.

Mathematical Emphasis At the beginning of each investigation, the Mathematical Emphasis section tells you what is most important for students to learn about during that investigation. Many of these understandings and processes are difficult and complex. Students gradually learn more and more about each idea over many years of schooling. Individual students will begin and end the unit with different levels of knowledge and skill, but all will gain greater knowledge about counting, collecting, sorting, classifying, and representing data.

"Not Brown Hair"

Throughout the *Investigations* curriculum, there are many opportunities for ongoing daily assessment as you observe, listen to, and interact with students at work. You can use almost any activity in this unit to assess your students' needs and strengths. Listed below are questions to help you focus your observations in each investigation. You may want to keep track of your observations for each student to help you plan your curriculum and monitor students' growth. Suggestions for documenting student growth can be found in the section About Assessment (p. I-8).

Investigation 1: How Many Are We?

■ What materials do students choose to represent the number of students in the classroom, and how do they use them?

■ How do students keep track of the items in their representations? Do the representations in fact account for everyone in the class?

■ Are students interested in how other classmates have represented the number of people in the class?

■ Do they use one-to-one correspondence when they count? If so, how many objects are they able to count accurately?

■ Do students recognize the one-to-one correspondence between the number of people in the class and the number of cubes in the nose tower? How do they show this?

■ What sort of statements do students make about the eye chart? Are they beginning to see that the chart offers information about the number of eyes and the number of people?

■ When students sort their self-portraits, what criteria do they use? Are they able to create two groups, one being a NOT group?

■ When students count the number of chairs in the classroom, are they able to compare this amount to the known information about the number of people? How do they compare the two amounts? Do they know which is more and which is less? Can they figure out how many more or less?

Investigation 2: What Did You Eat for Lunch?

■ How do students describe the groups they use for sorting? Can they explain their reasoning for making those groups?

■ Do students understand the concepts of *same* and *different*? Are they able to identify attributes of objects that are the same and attributes that are different? Are they able to explain their thinking?

■ Can students choose a category and sort a set of objects into two groups, one being a NOT group? If not, how do they group their objects? Are students comfortable sorting a small group of objects in more than one way?

Investigation 3: Collecting Data About Our Class

■ Are students able to figure out a workable plan for gathering data? How do they record people's responses? Do they have or want a system for keeping track of whom they have asked and whom they have not asked?

■ Are students able to count accurately the number of responses for each category of data?

■ Are students able to explain their survey results with such statements as "Most people in our class like carrots" or "More people have a pet than don't have a pet"?

■ Are students able to group objects that are alike in some way?

■ How do students describe the attributes they have chosen to make their groups?

■ Are students able to sort objects into two groups, one being a NOT group, or do they make many different groups?

■ What ideas are students using to make a representation that communicates the results of their surveys to others? Are their categories clear and understandable?

Investigation 4: Who's Here? Who's Not?

- Do students understand the problem that is posed? Can they explain it to another student?

- What materials do students choose and how do they use them?

- Do students use the total number of people in the class to help them solve the problem?

- What counting strategies, such as comparing quantities, counting on, or counting back, do students use to help solve this problem?

- How do students count and keep track of the data?

- Are students able to explain their strategy for solving the problem? Is their strategy evident from the representation they make?

Choosing Student Work to Save

As the unit ends, you might use one of the following options for creating a record of students' work.

- Look through any work samples that students have created during the unit and select a few examples to save in a portfolio or to share during parent conferences. For this unit, you might include students' representations for How Many Are We? and Pattern Block Grab; their recordings for Same and Different; their results from the Yes/No Surveys, and their strategies for the problem in Who's Here? Who's Not?

- Look back through your observation notes for each student. Depending on how you have organized this information, you might select a sample of observations that document student growth and understanding, or you may want to write a brief paragraph summarizing each students' work during the unit.

- Together with your students, write a group letter to families that describes the mathematical work students did during the unit. They might tell which activities they enjoyed most and what they think they learned from the work they did. In one classroom, the teacher prepared the students' letter on the computer and also included a few samples of work. Every child in the class signed the letter before it was copied and distributed to families.

In the *Investigations* curriculum, mathematical vocabulary is introduced naturally during the activities. We don't ask students to learn definitions of new terms; rather, they come to understand such words as *triangle, add, compare, data,* and *graph* by hearing them used frequently in discussion as they investigate new concepts. This approach is compatible with current theories of second-language acquisition, which emphasize the use of new vocabulary in meaningful contexts while students are actively involved with objects, pictures, and physical movement.

Listed below are some key words used in this unit that will not be new to most English speakers at this age level, but may be unfamiliar to students with limited English proficiency. You will want to spend additional time working on these words with your students who are learning English. If your students are working with a second-language teacher, you might enlist your colleague's aid in familiarizing students with these words, before and during this unit. In the classroom, look for opportunities for students to hear and use these words. Activities you can use to present the words are given in the appendix, Vocabulary Support for Second-Language Learners.

body parts (nose, eyes, legs, etc.) In Investigation 1, students work on one-to-one and two-to-one correspondence as they "count noses" in the classroom and then count eyes, legs, and other body parts that come in twos.

clothing and color names In Investigation 1, students draw self-portraits and then sort them according to such attributes as type and color of clothing and eye and hair color. In Investigation 2, they sort items of clothing in different ways.

sort, group, same, different Students sort items into groups throughout the unit, discussing whether the items are the same or different in particular ways.

typical lunch foods In Investigation 2, students identify their favorite lunch foods and then sort these into groups. You will need to identify common items that will likely be mentioned by your class and introduce this vocabulary.

Multicultural Extensions for All Students

Whenever possible, encourage students to share words, objects, customs, or any aspects of daily life from their own cultures and backgrounds that are relevant to the activities in this unit. For example:

■ In Investigation 2, What Did You Eat for Lunch?, students explore the favorite lunch foods of the people in their class. Encourage students to share favorite foods from a variety of cultures. If it is possible at your school, you might try preparing some of these foods with the students.

■ For the activity Boxes, Bottles, and Cans, students bring from home different containers to sort. Encourage them to bring in containers for products from other countries. The written language on the container might be one way to sort the items. They could also consider different ways to organize these items in the class grocery store.

■ In an activity called Clothing Sort, students sort items of clothing by size, color, function, and so forth. If possible, include clothing styles from different cultures. Students might enjoy contributing items of clothing and explaining to their classmates where the items originate and when people typically wear them.

Investigations

INVESTIGATION 1

How Many Are We?

Focus Time

How Many Are We? (p. 4)

In this investigation, students make several different representations of their class—the group of people for whom they will be collecting data over the entire unit. They begin by counting the people in the class and making individual recordings of their results.

Counting Noses, Counting Eyes (p. 16)

Students suggest ways of counting noses in the classroom. They take the count and make a representation of the result. Then they list body parts that come in twos and finish by making a class "eye chart."

Choice Time

Self-Portraits (p. 25)

Students create detailed self-portraits, which they sort into groups according to attributes such as hair color or types of clothing.

Counting Chairs (p. 28)

Students count chairs to determine whether there are enough for everyone in the class. They make a representation to show their work.

Pattern Block Grab (p. 30)

Students grab a handful of pattern blocks and then make a representation that shows how many and what kinds of blocks they grabbed.

Mathematical Emphasis

- Developing and using strategies for counting
- Relating counting to the quantity of items in a group
- Using one-to-one correspondence
- Exploring two-to-one correspondence
- Recording and representing data in a variety of ways
- Looking at different representations of the same data set
- Sorting objects into groups by attribute

Teacher Support

Teacher Notes

Dialogue Boxes

What to Plan Ahead of Time

Focus Time Materials

How Many Are We?

- Cubes, buttons, counters
- Art materials such as dot stickers, 1-inch squares of colored paper, crayons, markers, colored pencils, glue sticks
- Large drawing paper (at least 11 by 17 inches): 1 sheet per student

Counting Noses, Counting Eyes

- Interlocking cubes: 2 per student plus extras
- Index cards, 3 by 5 inches: 1 per student
- Crayons or markers
- Chart, 8 inches by about 6 feet (length varies with class size)
- Chart paper: 3 sheets
- Small mirrors to share (optional)
- Glue sticks or tape

Choice Time Materials

Self-Portraits

- Drawing paper (at least 6 by 9 inches): 1 per student plus extras
- Crayons or other drawing materials
- Small mirrors to share (optional)

Counting Chairs

- Clipboards: 1 per student (optional); can be made by attaching a sheet of paper to a book or stiff cardboard with a large paper clip, clothespin, or binder clip
- Unlined paper: 1 per student plus extras
- Counters: a large supply
- Art supplies

Pattern Block Grab

- Pattern blocks: 1 bucket per 4–6 students
- Unlined paper: 1 sheet per student
- Crayons or markers

Family Connection

- Family letter (p. 110): 1 per family, or *Investigations* at Home
- Counting Eyes at Home (p. 111): 1 per student, for optional homework

Preparation for Investigation 2

- Start collecting containers such as small boxes, empty plastic bottles, and canned goods for use in Investigation 2. To solicit help from families, duplicate and send home Help Stock Our Class Store (p. 112).

How Many Are We?

What Happens

As a whole group, students count the number of people in the class. Each student then creates his or her own representation of the count. Students might make a physical model with cubes, buttons, or counters, or they might show the information on paper with art materials. Their work focuses on:

- collecting data by counting
- representing data in a variety of ways
- looking at different representations of the same set of data

Materials and Preparation

- Gather materials for creating data representations, including both manipulative materials (cubes, buttons, counters of various kinds) and art materials (dot stickers, 1-inch squares of colored paper, crayons, markers, colored pencils, glue sticks).
- Make available a sheet of large drawing paper (at least 11 by 17 inches) for each student.

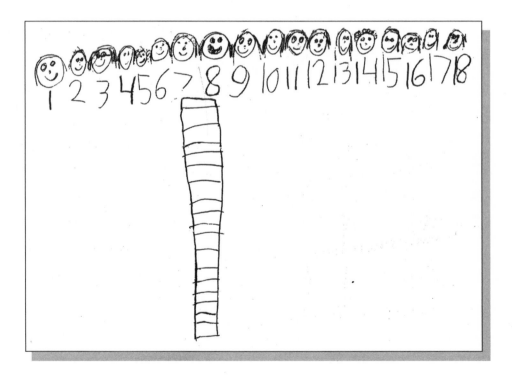

Counting the Class

Note: If your students are familiar with the classroom routine Attendance (p. 93), suggested for use all year, you can spend less time discussing ways to count the people in the class and move quickly to making representations of the count.

Introduce this activity by asking students to think about why it might be important to know how many people there are in the class.

In the next few weeks, we will be collecting a lot of information about ourselves. We can find out some important information by counting. Today we'll start by counting the number of people in this class. Can you think of any reason why you or I or other people might need to know how many of us there are?

Collect ideas from students, encouraging them to explain their thinking. The **Dialogue Box,** Why Do We Need to Know? (p. 9), offers the suggestions from one kindergarten class.

Next ask for ideas about how to count the people in the classroom. Depending on the time of year, the size of the class may already be quite familiar to your students. Even so, discussing ways to determine the size of a group is good preparation for making representations of that group. See the **Teacher Note,** How Many Are We? (p. 10), for one teacher's experience with the activity. If students already know how many people there are in the class, ask them to think of ways they could double-check that number.

Who can think of some different ways of counting how many of us there are? How can we make sure we count everyone, even the people who are absent?

Some students may suggest counting everyone in the room or counting the names on a class list. Ask them to think of ways to be sure of the count.

Suppose we try to count everyone in our class—how can we make sure that we don't count anyone twice? Who has a way that would help us keep track of which people we have counted? What about people who are absent today?

Kindergartners have offered the following ideas for keeping track of the count:

■ Count each student as he or she stands up or sits down. Add the absent people at the end.

■ Ea... ...ubes are collected and
pl... ...hen one cube is added for
e...

■ E... ...board. The teacher adds
a... ...counts the marks.

Ask students to explain why each method works. Encourage them to talk about whether they would get the same total each time they count. This idea is not obvious to many 5- and 6-year-olds and is an important aspect of learning how to count. See the **Teacher Note,** Counting Is More Than 1, 2, 3 (p. 12), for more on students' understandings about counting.

Try a few of the counting strategies that students suggest. When all the students agree on a total, post the figure.

There are 25 people in our class.

Activity

Representing the Count

Challenge students to find a way to show how many students there are in the class.

Each of you will find one way to show this information. We have lots of different materials you can use. Here is what's most important: Someone who knows nothing about our class should be able to look at what you made and tell how many of us there are.

Point out the available materials—various counters and art supplies—and ask for students' ideas about what they could make to show the information. The more materials you offer, the greater variety of representations students are likely to generate. The **Teacher Note,** Inventing Pictures of the Data (p. 13), explains the importance of letting students find their own ways to represent data.

Some students may build physical models to represent the number of children in the classroom. To keep a record of their work, ask these students to also draw a picture of their model. Then, as they tell you how they used the materials, note this on their paper.

For example, if a student builds a tower of 25 cubes, suggest drawing a picture of the tower, being sure to show each cube. Save the physical model until the class discussion. A student who has collected 25 beans or other replaceable items might glue them onto a sheet of paper for a permanent record.

Some students may want to write numerals to show how many are in the class. When this is the case, encourage them also to show how many *without* writing numbers, either on the same sheet or a new one.

The **Teacher Note,** From the Classroom: How Many Are We? (p. 10), describes the range of representations made by students in one class. See the **Teacher Note,** One-to-One Correspondence (p. 14), for more on students' strategies and their understanding of this activity.

Observing the Students

As students make their representations, circulate to ask about their work:

How do you know your model (or picture) shows exactly the number of students in the class? What does each cube (or button, or dot) stand for?

Consider their answers and also note the following:

- What materials do students choose to represent the number of people in the class, and how do they use them?
- How do students keep track of the items in their representations?
- How do students count the items in their representations? Do they compare this count to the known information about the number of people in the class?
- Do the representations in fact account for everyone in the class?
- Are students interested in how their classmates have represented the number of people in the class?

Not all students' representations will show the data accurately. Keep in mind that numbers in the 20's are very large for kindergartners, who are still in the process of developing successful strategies for counting and keeping track. Many students will believe that they have shown everyone in the class and will not seem to care that their model is not an accurate representation of the data. These students have yet to develop a solid understanding of larger numbers.

As students finish their work, suggest that they write or dictate a title. If you have enough space, display the representations.

Sharing Representations

Gather students in the display area for a brief discussion of their representations. If students are bringing their work to the meeting area, suggest that they sit in a circle and place their work in the center.

You've found many different ways to show information about how many people we are. Some of you used cubes, some used counters, some used pictures, and someone wrote all the names.

Ask a few volunteers to explain their work to the group. To highlight the variety of possibilities, choose students who used different materials and strategies. As each student shares, ask for a show of hands to see who else used the same materials for their representation.

Knowing exactly how many of us there are is going to be helpful during the next few weeks, as we collect different kinds of information about the people in our class.

Display as many of the representations as possible, or bind them into a book for future reference.

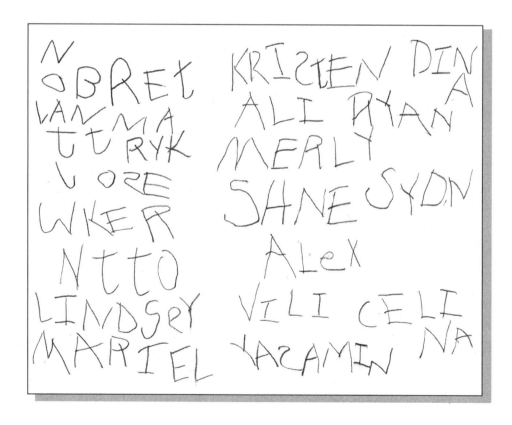

Why Do We Need to Know?

In this discussion, students offer a variety of reasons for counting the number of people in the class. The teacher is careful to give them the chance to expand on their ideas and is on the alert for important mathematical ideas that come up, such as when an exact count is needed and when an estimate will do.

Can you think of some times when people need to know how many of us there are?

Tiana: Maybe they need it for a certain reason.

For a certain reason? Can anyone think of a particular reason?

Thomas: They need to know how many people to get that many books.

For books?

Thomas: Like reading books.

Tarik: Yeah, like when everyone in my group got *A Kiss for Little Bear.*

OK. Who can think of another time?

Ida: In case we're taking a field trip and Tarik got left behind and we didn't know he was missing.

Did anyone ever use counting when they were on a trip?

Miyuki: Oh, like when we go on a trip and every time we got on and off the bus we counted off to make sure that we always had the same number.

Brendan: And my mom does that all the time.

What does she do, Brendan?

Brendan: Like when we go to the zoo and she goes 1, 2, 3, 4, 5, 6 all the time to make sure we are all there.

Xing-Qi: When we have a fire drill, the teachers are always counting us.

Yes, fire drills and field trips are important times when I need to know exactly how many of you there are. Can you think of any other times?

Gabriela: For sending the attendance to the office.

Tess: For bringing in snack—everyone should have a snack.

I remember when Thomas's dad brought in treats for his birthday.

Thomas: I told him how many of us there were. And we brought one for each person. And we brought some extras in case we had a visitor or something.

Felipe: And once we brought in apples, but we just brought in three big bags because we knew there would be extras. There were a lot of apples in each bag.

So sometimes it's important to know exactly how many we are so that we have enough of something for each person to have one, and sometimes we don't have to count exactly how many—we can think of an "about" amount.

Brendan: Things like snacks and stuff are important for everyone to have one, but sometimes there's things that you can share. Like books or puzzles or blocks—we share those things.

Because I have my students for less than three hours each day, I often have to spread out the Focus Time activities over two or three days. I decided to spread this activity [How Many Are We?] over three days. The first day I used our morning class meeting for Counting the Class because it connected to our daily discussion of who's here and who's not here. On the second day, after our morning meeting, I had the children move directly to the task of creating representations that showed the number of people in our classroom. In our daily schedule, we have a general choice period after a more structured work period, so students who finished early were able to transition immediately into Choice Time activities, and those who needed more time continued working. Our discussion of the students' representations took place at the morning meeting on the third day.

Before I began, I thought this activity would be too easy or too obvious for my students. We had been together for six months, and the number of students in the class, 23, was a firmly established fact, as were the number of boys and the number of girls. This was information that we talked about every day as we took attendance. For our class, then, the heart of this activity was not determining the size of our group, but representing that information. We spent a good deal of time sharing ideas for how the information could be shown either on paper or with objects. Having students talk about their ideas before they actually started to work helped launch them into the problem-solving process. I was a little surprised by how many different ideas the children had for figuring out the size of the group and making sure that we included everyone in the class.

A number of students attempted a drawing that included every person in the class. Two students succeeded in including everyone, while the others seemed to either lose track of the people in their representation or lose interest in drawing 23 figures. All of those students, however, were able to explain, "This is a drawing of the people in our class."

Other students used objects to represent the people in our class. A lot of them stacked interlocking cubes into a tower, and some used counters to show the 23 students. This was a challenging task for some students. While most could count by rote to 23, at least seven students had difficulty counting out 23 objects.

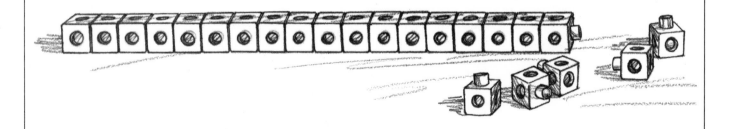

"This is the people in my class."

I did notice that the students who used cubes or counters were more accurate in representing 23 than the students who made drawings. I wonder if this was because the counters were easier to keep track of and required less effort than drawing 23 figures.

Most of the students used either drawings or counters, but there were other interesting approaches. One student made a list of everyone in our class by consulting the photographs we took at the beginning of the school year. Another wrote the numerals 1 through 23 to show the people in our class, and two others used dot stickers.

I gave a lot of thought to the matter of how to share the students' finished representations. I knew from experience that having 23 students "show and tell" would not be productive or informative for anyone. On the other hand, I also knew from past experience that kindergarten students can begin to have interesting mathematical discussions. For this first investigation, I decided to simply post the representations. I cleared the two walls that formed the corner of our meeting area so we were surrounded by different ways of representing the number of students. I held informal conversations with both individuals and small groups of students. Through this exhibit, the students were exposed to many different ways of displaying the same information. I hope they got some new ideas for making representations as well.

Counting is the basis for understanding our number system and for almost all the number work in the primary grades. It involves more than just knowing the number names, their sequence, and how to write each numeral. While it may seem simple, counting is actually quite complex and involves the interplay between the following skills and concepts.

Rote Counting Students need to know the number names and their order by rote; they learn this sequence by hearing others count and by counting themselves. However, just as saying the alphabet does not indicate that a student can use written language, being able to say "one, two, three, four, five, six, seven, eight, nine, ten" does not necessarily indicate that students know what those counting words mean. Students also need to use numbers in meaningful ways if they are to build an understanding of quantity and number relationships.

One-to-One Correspondence To count accurately, a student must know that one number name stands for one object that is counted. Often, when young children first begin to count, they do not connect the numbers in the "counting song" to the objects they are counting. Children learn about one-to-one correspondence through repeated opportunities to count sets of objects and to watch others as they count. One-to-one correspondence develops over time, with students first counting small groups of objects (up to five or six) accurately, and eventually larger groups.

Keeping Track Another important part of counting accurately is being able to keep track of what has been counted and what still remains to be counted. As students first begin to count sets of objects, they often count some objects more than once and skip other objects altogether. Students develop strategies for organizing and keeping track of a count as they realize the need and as they see others use such strategies.

Connecting Numbers to Quantities We use numbers both to count a set of objects and to describe the quantity of those objects. Many young students are still coordinating these two aspects of number—the *ordinal* sequence of the numbers with the *cardinal* meaning of those numbers. In other words, we get to 5 by counting in order, 1, 2, 3, 4, 5. In this sequence, 4 comes after 3, and 5 comes after 4. Understanding this aspect of number is connected to the one-to-one correspondence between the numbers we say and the objects we are counting. However, being able to count accurately using this ordinal sequence is not the same as knowing that when we are finished counting, the final number in our sequence tells the quantity of the things we have counted.

Conservation Conservation of number involves understanding that three is always three, whether it's three objects pushed or linked together, three objects spread apart in a line, or some other formation. As students learn to count, you will see many who do not yet understand this idea. They think that the larger the arrangement of objects, the more objects there are. Being able to conserve quantity is not a skill that can be taught; it is a cognitive process that develops as children grow and develop. This unit provides many opportunities for kindergartners to bump up against this important developmental milestone.

Counting by Groups Counting a set of objects by equal groups, such as 2's, requires that each of the steps mentioned above happens again, at a different level. First, students need to know the 2's sequence (2, 4, 6, 8 . . .) by rote. They need to realize that one number in this count represents two objects, and that each time they say a number they are adding another group of two to their count. Keeping track while counting by groups becomes a more complex task as well. Students begin to explore counting by 2's in this unit as they count the number of eyes in their class. However, most students will not count by groups in a meaningful way until first or second grade.

Inventing Pictures of the Data

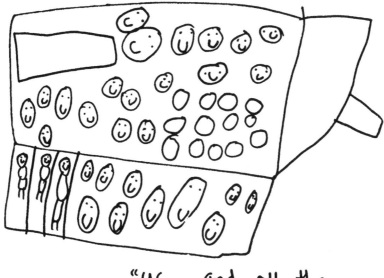

"us and all the people visiting today"

Two important aspects of representing data are (1) that the representation communicates information or "a story" about a situation or a group of people, and (2) that the author understands the representation well enough to explain it to others. When adults think about visual representations of data, they are likely to think in terms of such standard forms as charts, bar graphs, and line plots. However, when children are encouraged to invent their own ways of representing their data, they often come up with wonderfully individual pictures or unconventional graphs that help them communicate the meaning of the data.

This unit emphasizes the use of concrete materials and pictures to represent the data students collect. During the first investigation, students make representations that show the number of people in the classroom. Many kindergartners will use objects, such as counters or cube towers, to represent the data, while others will show this information in a pictorial way. When they represent similar data in Counting Noses, Counting Eyes, they are asked to use cubes to represent the number of noses in their class, and then to put together a collection of pictures to represent the number of eyes.

In the second investigation, students show their favorite part of lunch by drawing pictures of each piece of data. Then, working together as a whole class, they find their own ways to organize these data and put together a large representation that will somewhat resemble a pictorial bar graph.

Students' representations will not necessarily follow the conventions of graphing that adults use. Often the pictures vary in size and are not lined up evenly, making it difficult to count them quickly and to compare the sizes of different groups. These early attempts at representing data do, however, convey information in a way that is meaningful to the student and often to others as well.

Encourage students to find their own ways to show the data throughout this unit. When students are pushed to adopt the conventions of what graphs are "supposed to" look like, too often they produce graphs that, for them, do not communicate anything about their data. By inventing and constructing their own representations, students will become more familiar with their data and remain clear about what their picture or graph represents.

It is obvious to us as adults that if we put out a button for each student on the class list, there will be 25 buttons if there are 25 students. However, this correspondence is not always obvious to 5- and 6-year-olds. In the whole-class activity How Many Are We?, students are developing some very basic ideas about how a model—whether a set of pictures or a set of buttons—can represent another set of things, such as people in a class.

When one class worked on this activity, one boy carefully placed a button on top of each name on the class list and then rearranged the buttons in a long line across the table. He counted the buttons several times and was finally satisfied that there were 25.

What did you do with the buttons?

Carlo: I put a button for every name, and then I counted them and there was 25. But once I counted and there was only 23, so I counted them again. See, 1, 2, 3, 4, . . . , 23, 24, 25!

And what do those buttons tell you?

Carlo: There is one for every kid in the class.

How do you know?

Carlo: Because I put one on each name, and there's 25 names and 25 kids in our class, and so there's 25 buttons.

How do you know there are 25 names and buttons and kids?

Carlo: Because we've been counting the kids all year and there's 25 in our class, and the class list has everyone's name, and I put out one button for every name, and there's one name and one button for every kid.

Carlo's understanding of the correspondence of names to buttons to people is apparent from the way he relates what he knows about the number of students in his class to the names on the class list and to the buttons he placed on all the names. He expected there to be 25 buttons when he counted them. The fact that he miscounted the buttons but knew to count them again suggests that he understands one-to-one correspondence and the way counting gives information about the number of things in a group.

Justine used a similar approach to Carlo's, placing one shell on each name on the class list.

What did you use to show all the students in the class?

Justine: Shells.

And what do the shells tell you?

Justine: Um, I put one on everyone's name. And then I counted.

I wonder how many shells you have?

Justine [*shrugging her shoulders*]: I forget.

Is there a way you could figure that out?

Justine: Uh-huh. Count them. See, 1, 2, 3, 4, 5 . . . [*she counts all the shells, but occasionally loses track and arrives at 28*]. No, that's different. I think that's too much.

Too much what?

Justine: Too many shells. Last time I think I got 23 or 24.

Could we count them together? You move each shell as we count so we'll know what we've already counted.

The teacher helps Justine recount the shells. This time the girl carefully touches each shell and slides it to one side as she counts.

Justine: 1, 2, 3, . . . [*this time she accurately counts 25 shells*].

So what does that tell us?

Justine: That there's 25 shells?

Does it help you know how many people there are?

Justine: Um, 25? But I could count the names and really find out.

In this exchange, Justine is beginning to make sense of how a model can represent other things. While she seems to have a sense of the rote-counting sequence, her ability to keep track of larger numbers still seems a bit shaky. And although she is using an effective strategy (matching shells to names), she doesn't yet have a firm understanding of the idea that numbers represent quantities. Her comment that 28 seemed like too much suggests that she has a sense of what the number should be. By offering to recount together and suggesting moving the shells to keep track, the teacher gently supported Justine's counting strategies without being intrusive.

Counting Noses, Counting Eyes

What Happens

Students investigate how many noses there are in the classroom. They suggest a plan for counting, count noses, and double-check their results by making a tower of interlocking cubes, one cube per nose. They then make a list of body parts that come in twos. Working as a group, they construct a large display chart of all the eyes in the class. The students' work focuses on:

- matching items with a one-to-one correspondence
- matching items with a two-to-one correspondence
- using concrete materials to record and represent data
- making pictures to record and represent data

Materials and Preparation

- Have a bucket of interlocking cubes with enough to allow 2 cubes per student, plus extras.
- Provide an index card (3 by 5 inches) for each student, and crayons or markers for drawing eyes.
- Tape together sheets of paper or poster board to make a tall chart, approximately 8 inches wide by 6 feet high, for mounting class eye data. Have glue sticks or tape available.
- Have three sheets of chart paper or board space available for class lists.
- If you have small mirrors, these are useful (but optional) when students are drawing their own eyes.

How Many Noses?

Open this activity with a discussion of the expression "counting noses."

A friend of mine had a big picnic at her house. She told me that she needed to know how many cups to bring outside, so before everybody sat down to eat, she "counted noses." What do you think she meant by that?

After students have shared their ideas, be sure everyone understands that the expression "counting noses" means finding out how many people there are.

Suppose we counted noses in our classroom. How many noses do you think there would be?

Some students, knowing that there are 25 children in the class, may be very sure that there are 25 noses. Others may be less certain or may not connect their previous experience with this new way of looking at the question. As students offer ideas about how many noses there are, encourage them to explain their reasoning.

Ask how the class could find out for sure how many noses there are in the room. Some students may suggest counting actual noses; others may suggest using a visual display such as a class photo, or a piece of information such as a class list. Help the class decide who should be included in the count—only students who are present? both present and absent students? adults, as well as students? Then choose one proposed method and use it to count noses.

Count noses

After the count, explain that students will use interlocking cubes to make a representation of the information they just gathered. Pass around a bucket of cubes so each student can take one. Ask students to make a "tower of noses" by snapping their cubes together, one at a time. As students add their cube to the class tower, they count off—the first student saying "one," the second saying "two," and so on. If you have agreed to include absent students in the count, add their cubes at the end.

Give one cube for each.
Nose Tower count-off as put on
How many cubes?

When the tower is complete, ask students how many cubes are in it and how they know. It may not be obvious to everyone that the number of cubes in the tower is the same as the number of students in the class. Listen for comments that suggest students are making a one-to-one correspondence between noses (people) and cubes.

When students agree on the number of noses, write this information on the board or on a sheet of chart paper.

Chart Noses #

If we know that there are 25 noses in our class, *what else* do we know there are 25 of?

Add students' ideas to make a data chart. Add a sketch to help students identify each new word.

Make data chart

There are 25 noses in our class.

There are 25 heads in our class.

There are 25 chins in our class.

There are 25 mouths in our class.

There are 25 hearts in our class.

Note that this activity might evoke sensitive issues in some classrooms. See the **Teacher Note,** Dealing with Sensitive Issues (p. 33).

During this activity, if anyone suggests things that people have *more* than one of, such as ears, legs, teeth, hair, fingers, or eyes, begin a second list of these on a separate sheet of chart paper. You can use this list to initiate the next activity.

Observing the Students

To monitor students' understanding during this discussion of counting noses, consider the following:

- Do students recognize the one-to-one correspondence between the number of children in the class and the number of cubes in the nose tower? How do they show this?
- Do they generalize this information to other body parts that they have one of, such as head, mouth, and so on?

How Many Eyes?

Focus students' attention on the second list you started, showing parts of the body we have more than one of.

We all have one nose, but there are some things on our body that come in twos. Who can think of some of those?

As students name or point out body parts that come in pairs, highlight them with a circle or a check mark. Add to the list any new ones that students name. Be sure that eyes are listed.

Suppose we wanted to count how many eyes there are in the classroom. How could we do that so we would have the exact number of eyes?

Accept as many different counting strategies as students suggest. Encourage students to think of ways to keep track of what has and has not been counted.

Some students may relate the number of eyes to the previous activity of counting noses. Listen for phrases such as *twice as many, double the number, two for each.* These are important indicators that students are beginning to develop an understanding of two-to-one correspondence, even though few kindergartners will be able to double the number of noses in the classroom. Some students might suggest counting by 2's as a strategy for counting the number of eyes. Although this is a valid strategy, kindergartners are not likely to be able to use it in a meaningful way.

The **Teacher Note,** Two-to-One Correspondence (p. 34), and the **Dialogue Box,** Counting Eyes (p. 35), offer information about making a bridge between counting by 1's and counting by 2's, and discuss counting strategies your students might suggest.

Choose one of the suggested methods to count the eyes in your class. In deciding whose eyes should be counted, follow the same guidelines that the class agreed on for the nose count.

It's a good idea to link the counting of each eye with some physical movement to help students associate the numbers with the objects being counted. It's also helpful to double-check the count using a different strategy. When the count is complete, write this information on chart paper. As with the "nose" list, extend this "eye" list with other body parts that come in twos.

If we each have 2 eyes and there are 50 eyes in our classroom, how many legs do you think there are in our classroom? How could we check that information?

Take a count of legs and add this information to the data chart. Include a picture to represent each part counted.

There are 50 eyes in our class.

There are 50 legs in our class.

There are 50 elbows in our class.

Counting other body parts can be an ongoing activity during future whole-class meetings. If your students generate a lot of strategies for counting, list their ideas on chart paper so they can choose different strategies for future counts. Kindergartners typically like strategies that involve physical movement, such as raising both hands and putting them down as they are counted, or stamping each foot as it is counted.

Making a Class "Eye Chart"

Explain that the class is now going to work together to represent the eye data. That is, they will make a picture that shows the information about how many eyes there are in the class. Distribute the index cards or slips of paper and drawing materials for each student to make a picture of his or her own eyes. If you have mirrors available, students can research the shape of their eyes, the color, and the parts (pupil, lid, lashes).

To collect the eye data, post vertically the long paper strip you have prepared in advance. As students finish their eye cards, they glue or tape them onto this strip, starting at the bottom, to make a tall tower of eye cards. Note that this is not to be a graph of categories, such as eye colors, but rather a simple representation of all the eyes in the classroom. When all the cards have been added, ask students to suggest a name for the chart and write it at the top of the paper. Then discuss ways to count all the eyes shown.

Suppose we were going to count the number of eyes on our eye chart. How many eyes do you think there are?

Some students are likely to connect this information to the eye count that they just completed, although not all kindergartners will make this association. Ask the class to count with you as you point to each eye on the chart. Many students would not be able to count this high on their own; by counting together, everyone gets experience with counting to a relatively high number. Verify the result of the count with the information you wrote on chart paper earlier.

Suppose one of your parents or another teacher from our school came into our classroom and looked at our eye chart. What kind of information could they get from it?

If no one mentions the number of people in the class, ask:

Could they tell how many people are in our class just by looking at the chart? How could they figure that out?

Some kindergartners will make the connection between the number of students in class and the number of cards on the chart. They are beginning to see that a model can also be a representation of real data and that actual things like people or eyes can be represented with concrete materials. In addition, they are beginning to see that each card represents one person and more than one eye. This is a step toward abstract thinking that not all children of this age are ready to take. Repeated experiences with counting real objects and representing them with pictures or other concrete objects will help students to begin to understand these more abstract ideas about representing data.

Could someone tell how many eyes there are in our class just by looking at the chart? How could they figure out that information?

Observing the Students

Consider the following during the discussion of number of eyes in the class:

- After counting eyes, do students generalize this information to other body parts that come in twos?
- What sort of statements do students make about the eye chart? Are they beginning to see that the chart offers information about both the number of eyes *and* the number of people?

Focus Time Follow-Up

Homework

Family Connection Send home the signed family letter or the *Investigations* at Home booklet to introduce your work in this data unit.

Eyes at Home For optional homework, each student takes home a copy of the letter Counting Eyes at Home (p. 111). You might also send home drawing paper. Students should bring back to class a representation of the number of eyes in their home. Encourage them to think about how to show this information so someone looking at their picture would know how many people live at their house, how many eyes there are, and what color the people's eyes are. Emphasize to students that they can represent these data in any way they like that makes sense to them; the "eye chart" they made in class is just one way.

Post students' representations in a central spot and spend some time discussing the various ways students chose to represent their data.

Preparation for Investigation 2 Several Choice Time activities in Investigation 2 (Boxes, Bottles, and Cans; The Grocery Store; and Clothing Sort) require some advance preparation. At this time you should start collecting empty plastic bottles, empty boxes, unopened cans, and paper or plastic bags for use in a sorting activity and in a class grocery store. Copy and send home the letter Help Stock Our Class Store (p. 112) if you want family help in collecting these items.

You will also need similar items of clothing in three distinct sizes; refer to page 51 for details. You might ask a parent to help you assemble these sets.

 **Choice Time**

Three Choices To review the use of Choice Time in the *Investigations* curriculum, see the **Teacher Note,** About Choice Time (p. 86).

During the first Choice Time of this unit, students work with activities that offer experience with sorting, counting, and representing data. With Self-Portraits (p. 25), students each contribute to another way of representing their whole class and find ways to sort the class data into groups. On subsequent days you can introduce Counting Chairs (p. 28) and Pattern Block Grab (p. 30).

Self-Portraits

Counting Chairs

Pattern Block Grab

Self-Portraits

What Happens

Students create head-to-toe self-portraits, specifically portraying important features such as hair color, eye color, hair style, and missing teeth, as well as what kind of clothing they are wearing. Working in small groups, they then sort these pictures according to certain attributes they can identify in the drawings. Their work focuses on:

- describing attributes
- recording information in a picture
- sorting into groups by attribute

Materials and Preparation

- Have available a sheet of drawing paper for each student, plus some extras. If you have a camera for taking snapshots, an alternative approach is to use photographs instead of self-portraits for sorting and counting.
- Provide drawing materials that include a variety of colors; crayons usually offer the most flexibility.
- If you have mirrors, make these available for students to share.

Activity

This activity has two parts: First students work individually to create detailed self-portraits; then they work in small groups to sort those portraits. Plan to introduce the second part of the activity after students have completed their portraits.

Creating Self-Portraits Introduce the activity by asking students to describe you.

Pretend that you are talking to someone who does not know me, and you are telling them what I look like. Look very carefully. How would you describe me—the way I look and what I am wearing—so this person could picture me?

After students have described you, you might have them describe one or two of their classmates to give them more practice in looking closely at physical characteristics and clothing. Then explain that it's time to look closely at themselves and make self-portraits—pictures of themselves—that show what they look like.

Be sure to put lots of details in your picture of yourself. Your picture should show the color of your hair, the color of your eyes, and the color of your skin. Also put in special things like glasses or missing teeth. Draw the clothes you are wearing today. When your self-portraits are finished, we should be able to match each one to the right person.

Make the paper and drawing materials available. You may want students to make their self-portraits as a whole class rather than during Choice Time. Either way, give a time limit for completing the portraits so everyone's picture will be available for the sorting activity.

Sorting the Portraits To introduce the sorting part of the activity, gather students in a circle with seven or eight finished portraits in the center. Identify one attribute that several portraits share.

As I was looking at your self-portraits, I noticed some things that are *the same* about some of the pictures. For example, the people in three of these pictures [are wearing shorts]. Let's see if we can put these portraits into two groups. One group will be the people who [are WEARING SHORTS], and the other will be the people who [are NOT WEARING SHORTS].

With the students' help, sort the pictures into two groups. It is likely that some portraits will not clearly show this information. Ask students for their ideas about what to do with these pictures. They may suggest putting the pictures in a third group—a CAN'T TELL group. As you sort the pictures, try to display them side by side rather than stacked, so that the chosen attribute remains visible.

When students have sorted the portraits into groups, ask them to count the total number of portraits again, to reinforce the one-to-one correspondence between the students in the class and the individual pieces of data (the self-portraits).

After sorting the portraits once as a whole-group, help the class brainstorm some other characteristics they could use for sorting when they work in small groups. Explain that they can use any of these ideas for sorting portraits in their small groups during Choice Time.

Observing the Students

Consider the following as you watch students sorting the self-portraits.

- When students sort their self-portraits, what criteria do they use?
- Are students able to create at least two groups, one being a NOT group?
- Do students sort using more than two groups, for example, according to eye color or hair color?
- Do students notice that pictures can belong in more than one group? For example, a portrait that appears in the SHORTS group for a WEARING SHORTS/NOT WEARING SHORTS sort might also be placed in a BROWN HAIR group for a hair-color sort.

Counting Chairs

What Happens

Students work individually to count the chairs in the classroom. Before they begin, they decide on a way to keep track of their count. They then determine if there are enough chairs for everyone in the room by comparing the number of chairs to the number of people, and they represent how many extra chairs there are or how many more chairs are needed. Their work focuses on:

- counting a set of objects
- using one-to-one correspondence to match two sets of objects
- keeping track of data
- comparing two sets of data

Materials and Preparation

- Make available a large quantity of counters, such as buttons or cubes.
- Provide unlined paper and drawing materials both for collecting data and for making representations of the data. Clipboards are useful since students need to keep track of data while they move around the room; these can be handmade (see p. 3).

Activity

Note: This activity works best when limited to three or four students at a time.

To introduce the activity, ask students how many chairs they think you have in the classroom. Record their guesses on the board or chart paper.

Do you think there are enough chairs for everyone to have one? How do you know? What if we wanted to have one chair for every person? How many chairs would we need?

Suppose we wanted to find out exactly how many chairs there are in our room. How could we do that?

After a few students have shared their ideas, explain that counting the chairs in the classroom is a Choice Time activity. Each of them should decide on a way to count the chairs, take the count, and then record the information on paper.

Think about how you'll keep track of your count while you are counting the chairs. You might use a sheet of paper, or you might use counters like cubes or buttons. You can use anything in the classroom to help you keep track.

When you have finished your count, figure out if there are enough chairs for every person in our class to have one. Are there any extra chairs? Or do we need more chairs? How would you figure this out?

Students can use any materials in the classroom as they work on this problem. Encourage them to make a model or draw a picture to show how they solved the problem.

Observing the Students

Consider the following as you observe students at work on Counting Chairs.

- How do students count the number of chairs?
- Do students have a system for keeping track of what they have or have not counted, or do they count randomly?
- Do students use counters or other materials to help them keep track as they count?
- How do students record the chair data? Do they use pictures? tallies? numerals?
- How do students compare the number of chairs to the number of people in the class? Do they use counters? tallies? numerals? fingers?
- How do students figure out how many more or fewer chairs they would need for everyone to have exactly one chair?

Sharing Our Work Plan to hold a short discussion after most students have worked on this activity, so they can share their techniques for counting and their results with the rest of the class. Encourage them to talk about what was hard about counting the chairs. Ask them also to think about how they kept track while they were counting, and why this was important.

Variation

Students count other objects in the classroom and compare those numbers to the number of people in class. Keep track of this information on a chart. So, for example, a chart might list 25 people, 28 chairs, 10 tables, and 26 cubbies.

Pattern Block Grab

What Happens

Students make a representation of the pattern blocks that they are able to grab in one handful. Their representation should show the types of blocks they grabbed, how many of each, and how many in all. Their work focuses on:

- counting items in a data set
- representing a set of data

Materials and Preparation

- Divide pattern blocks into containers. Provide 1 container for each 2–3 students working at this activity.
- Provide paper and crayons or markers for students' representations.

Activity

To introduce this activity, gather students around a container of pattern blocks.

How many pattern blocks do you suppose I can pick up with one hand? Who has an estimate of how many blocks I can grab?

Solicit a few responses from students and then take a handful of blocks. Lay them out and ask different students to count each type of block, but do not record these amounts. Then ask someone to count how many blocks there are in all.

When you try Pattern Block Grab during Choice Time, you're going to grab a handful of blocks and count them. After you have figured out how many blocks you grabbed, you will make a representation that shows how many of each kind of block you grabbed. You can use words or numbers or pictures to help you show what was in your handful. Who has an idea about how you could record this information on paper?

Ask two or three students to share their ideas for recording, but do not demonstrate any of those methods now. This encourages students to explore a variety of ways to represent the data.

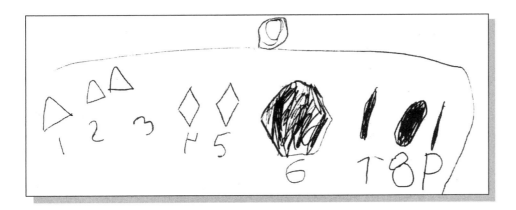

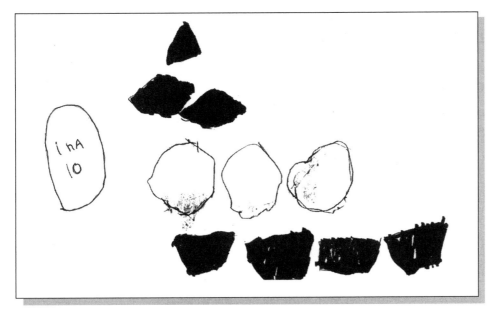

Observing the Students

Consider the following as you watch students at work on Pattern Block Grab.

- Do students organize their blocks in any way? If so, what strategy do they use?
- How do students count? Do they have a way of keeping track of the blocks they have counted? Do they count accurately?
- How do students represent their handful of blocks? Do they show each block, or do they use symbols such as tally marks or numerals?
- Are students using an organizational system in their representations so that you can quickly see how many of each kind of block they grabbed?

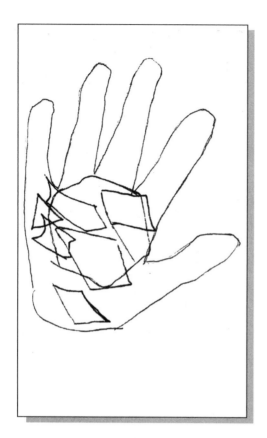

When a few students have completed the activity, they can share their representations during a class meeting and discuss different ways of recording the data. A student should have the option of explaining his or her own representation or letting classmates try to explain it.

Variation

Encourage students to do this activity twice and compare the numbers of blocks in the two handfuls. After grabbing one handful, organizing the blocks, and counting them, they leave those blocks on the table. They then grab another handful of blocks to organize and count. (While some students might be able to compare the two quantities mentally, most students will benefit from seeing both handfuls on the table at the same time.)

Observe how students compare the two amounts. Do they line up the two sets of blocks and make a one-to-one comparison? Do they place one set of blocks on top of the other?

Ask students to make a representation of their two handfuls, showing how they compared the blocks.

Dealing with Sensitive Issues

Some sensitive issues may arise when students are doing the activities in Counting Noses, Counting Eyes. Students who wear glasses may be uncomfortable with the focus on eyes in the classroom. Also, there may be some general silliness about the body as students brainstorm lists of other things that come in ones and twos. You will have to handle these remarks according to your own and your school's approach. In field-test classes, students were so engaged in the mathematics of the activity that the discussion of private parts of the body never arose. However, you might want to consider in advance how to keep the focus on the mathematics.

Another issue may arise in classrooms with a student who does not have the usual number of body parts (for example, a child who is missing an arm). If this is the case in your classroom, you will have already talked with your class about the student's special needs, so that some matter-of-factness toward the child's differences has been established.

In the activity Counting Noses, Counting Eyes, any differences should be included in the discussion as a mathematical issue. For example, you might say, "If we are going to count arms and Jesse has one arm, how can we make sure we get the right count?"

Depending on your own style and the atmosphere in the class, you can even make this a highlight of the mathematics: "We know we have 50 eyes, but Seth thinks something different will happen when we count arms. Who can predict how many arms we will have?" Such discussions are often much more uncomfortable for adults than for students, including the student who is different, who is likely to be genuinely interested in such a problem.

The relationships of *half* and *double* are key mathematical ideas. The two-to-one correspondence that students have noticed on their own bodies (with eyes, ears, hands, and such), as well as in sharing activities ("two for you, two for me"), will lead them to critical ideas about multiplication, division, and ratios. Forming pairs and counting by 2's is also connected to later work in place value, when students discover that a group of things can be counted as one group and, at the same time, retain the value of the number of items in it (one group of ten and ten ones, for example).

Counting by groups of two is a challenging task for most kindergartners. In fact, the concept will not be firmly understood by most children until second or third grade. Just as young children learn to chant the names of the numbers from 1 to 10 long before they can accurately count objects and have an understanding of quantity, so too they learn the counting-by-2's chant "2, 4, 6, 8" without understanding how it relates to counting. In fact, most young students cannot go beyond 8, and they often relate that sequence of numbers to the familiar chant "2, 4, 6, 8. Who do we appreciate?" rather than to sets of two objects.

Kindergarten and first grade students will begin to understand the two-to-one relationship as they identify things that come in twos and talk about quantities as being *twice as much* or *double the amount*. Listen for remarks like these, which indicate students' growing understanding:

"We have twice as many eyes as noses."

"If you only counted one eye for everyone, that would be like noses. But eyes are double."

"You have to add 25 two times because you have two eyes for each person."

In kindergarten, the major emphasis in counting should be on developing sound and effective strategies for counting by 1's. You can, however, model situations so that students begin to see concrete ways of representing pairs. For example, when students are using the class eye chart to count the total number of eyes, they see two eyes on each card, but they are still counting by 1's. The rhythm of the counting sequence can be used to point out something special about this count. As you point to each eye and count, you can emphasize every second number: "One, *two,* three, *four,* five, *six* . . . "

To emphasize the two-to-one correspondence of eyes to people, students could take two interlocking cubes, one color for their right eye and another color for their left. Make a tower of right-eye cubes and a tower of left-eye cubes; then attach the two towers side by side so students can see them as one set of data. These towers can then be compared to the cube "tower of noses," with students noting that now there are twice as many towers (and cubes) and twice as many eyes.

As students count the eyes on the eye chart and make eye towers, they are seeing and using concrete models that represent the two-to-one relationship. Repeated experiences with models and opportunities to count by groups of two will reinforce students' understanding of two-to-one correspondence.

Counting Eyes

During a Focus Time meeting, these kindergartners have already "counted noses." In this dialogue they are considering the question of how many eyes are in their classroom.

Suppose we wanted to count how many eyes there are. How could we do that so we would have the exact number of eyes?

Alexa: We could count them. I could go around and say "1, 2, 3, 4," like we do for attendance.

Charlotte: You'd have to be careful that you don't poke some person's eye when you counted.

Oscar: We could take cubes, like when we counted our noses. Each person could take a cube.

Charlotte: It'd be different. You have to take two cubes.

Why would each person have to take two cubes?

Charlotte: Because we have two eyes!

Alexa: I think we should just go around and say "1, 2, 3."

Kadim: Have each person say their own number. Like I would say "1, 2," and Alexa would say "3, 4" because those are her eyes.

Suppose we went around the circle and counted each person's eyes. Is there some way that we could keep track of whose eyes we have counted and whose eyes we have not counted?

Jacob: We could stand up like we do sometimes for attendance. Then when you count your eyes, you sit down.

Renata: We could close our eyes once the person counted our eyes.

Jacob: I think we should just sit down 'cause everyone would end up with their eyes closed, and you might get dizzy and fall over or something.

Jacob suggested having people sit down, and Renata suggested closing your eyes. Once everyone was sitting down, or once everyone had their eyes closed, what would we know then?

Alexa: Well, if you had your eyes closed, you wouldn't know when you were finished.

I'm not sure I understand.

Alexa: You couldn't see, so how would we know when everyone had counted unless you peeked, like this *[squinting]*. Then you could tell when you were finished.

So we would have to know when we were finished counting. Any other ideas?

Oscar: If everyone was sitting down, then you would know that you counted everyone's eyes.

So these are ways of keeping track. Let's choose one to try and then we can choose another one to double-check our count.

Teacher Support ■ **35**

What Did You Eat for Lunch?

Focus Time

What Did You Eat for Lunch? (p. 38)

In this investigation, students look closely at the attributes of objects and then use this information to sort the objects into groups. They begin by collecting categorical data about lunch foods and discussing various ways to group their data. They choose one way and make a large representation of their favorite lunch foods.

Choice Time

Same and Different (p. 44)

Working in pairs, students choose two similar objects and determine how they are the same and how they are different from each other.

Boxes, Bottles, and Cans (p. 46)

Students sort sets of containers into two categories: those that have a particular attribute and those that do not (the NOT group).

The Grocery Store (p. 48)

Sudents find ways to organize empty grocery containers and shelve them by categories. They take turns shopping and working in the store, helping to keep the stock organized.

Clothing Sort (p. 51)

Students work in small groups to sort the contents of a bag of clothing in different ways, such as by size, color, or function.

Mathematical Emphasis

- Collecting, recording, and representing data
- Organizing a set of data in more than one way
- Noting the similarities and differences in a group of related objects
- Sorting objects by attribute into two groups
- Finding different ways to sort and classify a group of objects
- Discussing the information in a data representation

Teacher Support

Teacher Notes

Choosing Categories (p. 53)

Questions That Promote Data Analysis (p. 54)

Dialogue Box

But My Peach Was Sweet (p. 55)

What to Plan Ahead of Time

Focus Time Materials

What Did You Eat for Lunch?

- *This Is the Way We Eat Our Lunch* by Edith Baer (Scholastic, 1995) (optional)
- Unlined paper: 1 sheet per student
- Index cards, 5 by 8 inches (or half sheets of paper): 1 per student
- Length of butcher paper or other large sheet for mounting lunch data cards
- Glue sticks or tape
- Chart paper

Choice Time Materials

Same and Different

- Pairs of similar objects, such as two different shoes, a wooden block and a plastic block, two different books, a cereal box and a tissue box. Assemble 7–8 pairs, each in a resealable bag or small box.
- Student Sheet 1, Same and Different (p. 113): 1 per pair

Boxes, Bottles, and Cans

- Small boxes, empty plastic bottles, and unopened cans: at least 8–10 of each
- Larger boxes for storage: 1 for each set of containers

The Grocery Store

- A wide variety of empty grocery item containers
- Index cards or small slips of paper for labeling the grocery shelves
- Chart paper: 1 sheet

Clothing Sort

- Similar items of clothing in each of three distinct sizes: infant or toddler, kindergarten-age child, and adult (shirts, pants, socks, shoes, hats, sweaters, mittens)
- Large box to store clothing

What Did You Eat for Lunch?

What Happens

After reading together *This Is the Way We Eat Our Lunch,* students collect data about their own lunch foods. Each student chooses his or her favorite part of the day's lunch; then the whole group discusses categories for these foods. Using one set of categories, the class sorts their favorite foods to create a large pictorial data chart. The students' work focuses on:

- collecting data
- sorting data according to common attributes
- organizing and representing categorical data
- discussing what a data representation shows

Materials and Preparation

- If possible, obtain a copy of *This Is the Way We Eat Our Lunch* by Edith Baer.
- Have several sheets of chart paper or board space available for making lists.
- Have one sheet of unlined paper and one 5-by-8-inch index card or half sheet of paper for each student, plus crayons or markers.
- Prepare a large sheet of paper (such as butcher paper) for mounting students' lunch data cards. The size you need will vary depending on the number of data pieces you have and the number of categories students choose. Have glue sticks or tape available.

oranges

peanut butter and jelly sandwich

salami

spaghetti

Favorite Lunch Foods

This Is the Way We Eat Our Lunch is a journey around the world, looking at different foods children eat for lunch. Read this book to your class as an entry point into collecting data about their own lunch foods. If you do not have the book, simply introduce this activity with a discussion.

People eat lots of different things for lunch, and lunch can have a lot of different parts to it. For example, sometimes my lunch is [a salad, yogurt, juice, and a cookie]. Sometimes it's [a sandwich, an apple, and milk]. What do you eat for lunch?

If your students all have the same school lunch, suggest that they think about what they eat for lunch at home, or the meals that are served at school on different days. On the board or chart paper, list the foods that students name. They will refer to this list later in the session.

at home?
Shared Writing
List foods - picture

Today we are going to collect some information about the foods we eat for lunch. We will use this information to make a chart of our favorite lunch foods.

The first thing you will do is make a picture of everything you might eat and drink for lunch on one particular day. After you have drawn your picture, we'll write the name of each food. You can use our class list of lunch foods to help you, or ask me for help.

1st step

Distribute unlined paper to each student. As the students work, remind them to think about all the different parts of their lunch. Ask questions as needed to help them remember everything they usually eat for lunch.

Do you have something to drink? Do you have any fruit or vegetables? Do you have dessert?

Question to get all details of lunch possibilities

When students have finished their drawings, organize the class into pairs or threes to share their lunch information with each other.

Groups of 3

With your partner (or small group), take turns explaining the picture you drew. If you realize that you forgot to put something on your sheet, don't worry—you can add that information later.

step 2

After students have shared their drawings, the next task is to identify the favorite part of their lunch.

You all had lots of delicious things in your lunches—it made me hungry! Now let's think about your very favorite part of lunch. Of all the things you drew on your paper—all the different things you have for lunch— which one is your favorite?

Favorite

Handwritten margin notes: Tell partners

Handwritten margin notes: Index Card to draw favorite part

Suggest that students tell their partners which is their favorite part of lunch.

I'm going to give each of you a card. Choose your favorite part of lunch and draw a picture of it on this card. Label your picture with a word. (You can look for the word on your bigger lunch picture, or ask me for help.)

Distribute the index cards or half sheets of paper. Point out that students should orient the cards horizontally to draw their favorite foods; having each piece of data the same shape helps when putting together the class data chart.

Sorting the Lunch Foods

Handwritten margin notes: HEAD COUNT

Gather students together with their completed cards showing favorite lunch foods. Begin by having students count off to determine the number in the group.

If everyone who is here today has a lunch card showing a favorite lunch food, how many cards do you think there are? How do you know?

As students share their ideas, listen for phrases that suggest they are working with one-to-one correspondence—that is, thinking in terms of one person/one card. Some might notice that this exercise is similar to counting noses. Confirm the number of lunch cards by counting them.

Handwritten margin notes: Share

Quickly go around the circle as students tell what food they drew on their card.

Handwritten margin notes: Sort, put into groups to discuss

Are most of our favorite foods the same or different? Can you tell? It might be easier to talk about our favorite foods if we put them into groups. Do you see a way that some of these foods go together as a group?

Handwritten margin notes: List Categories

List students' suggestions on chart paper or the board so that you can refer to their ideas later. Kindergartners are likely to begin by grouping things that are exactly the same so they have, for example, a PIZZA group, a PEANUT BUTTER SANDWICH group, a MACARONI AND CHEESE group, an APPLE group, and a POTATO CHIP group. This approach usually results in a lot of categories with only a few items in each. Nevertheless, it is important to let students participate in determining the categories for their lunch foods, as is discussed in the **Teacher Note**, Choosing Categories (p. 53).

Some more general ways that kindergartners have suggested categorizing their favorite lunch foods are these:

Suggestion

- healthy things/not healthy things
- dessert/drinks/sandwiches
- fruit/vegetables/things you drink/things with bread/cookies and cakes

The **Dialogue Box,** But My Peach Was Sweet (p. 55), illustrates the discussion of possible categories in one kindergarten class.

If students are having a difficult time thinking of categories, you might make suggestions.

Suppose one of our groups was SWEET THINGS. What foods do you think would go in this group? . . . How could we group the other foods that are *not* SWEET THINGS? What could we call this other group (or groups)?

To help students think about broader categories, plan to sort their lunch cards in several different ways. For the first sort, choose one set of categories from the list of student suggestions. Students might arrange their cards in groups in the middle of the circle, or they could take their cards and sit together in groups as a category is suggested.

When each sort is complete, ask students to comment on the results. Interpreting the data once they have been organized is an important part of working with data. Even the youngest students are able to think about what their data represent. You can encourage students to comment on the data in a *quantitative* way with questions like these:

How many people chose fruit as the favorite part of their lunch? How many people chose pizza as their favorite part?

Most students are inclined to notice quantitative information on graphs and representations, such as how many people liked a particular food. To help them see the important *qualitative* information, you can ask questions like these:

Can you say one thing about our favorite part of our lunches? What do you think is interesting about our favorite foods?

Encourage them as necessary with your own observations. You might, for example, note all the different kinds of fruit that people like, or express surprise that everyone didn't list dessert as their favorite part of lunch. The **Teacher Note**, Questions That Promote Data Analysis (p. 54), offers more information about involving kindergartners in such discussions.

When students have had the chance to sort the data in a few different ways and to discuss the results, either you or the class as a whole chooses one set of categories to use for a large class representation of the data.

You have a lot of good ideas for organizing the information about the favorite part of our lunches. Now we're going to choose one way to sort the foods and glue our cards down on paper so that we can save our representation. It seems that a lot of people were thinking about [dessert and sweet things], so let's use the groups [DESSERT and NOT DESSERT] in our representation.

Show students the large paper you have prepared for this data chart. Write the categories at the bottom.

We are going to organize our lunch cards on this paper. I have written *Dessert* and *Not Dessert* at the bottom. Think about the food that is on your lunch card and decide which group it belongs in.

A few at a time, students place their cards in the section they choose. Have available glue sticks or tape. Encourage students to make columns by placing each card above the previous one in their category. There may be some discussion among students as to which category is the right one for certain foods. This is one of the important issues in organizing categorical data. It's a good idea to let each student decide where to place his or her card.

[handwritten margin note: select. Class categories) to show. representation]

[handwritten margin note: Each child should place his own card]

When the chart is finished, ask students to tell you about the representation. Record their observations on another sheet of chart paper. At the end of this session, find a place to post both the large data chart and the list of student observations.

Focus Time Follow-Up

Shoe Data Many kindergarten students enjoy looking at and sorting the shoes they are wearing. The book *Shoes* by Elizabeth Winthrop (Harper and Row, 1986) is a good accompaniment to this exploration. Students might make a shoe card by drawing a picture of the shoe they are wearing today or their favorite shoe—or they can sort their actual shoes. Involve students in thinking about different ways the shoes can be grouped (color, style, laces, and so on). Students then use their shoe cards or actual shoes to make a representation of their data in chart form.

 **Extension**

Four Choices To follow the Focus Time survey of favorite lunch foods, the Choice Time activities give students experience in deciding on categories, sorting, and making representations. In Same and Different (p. 44), students look for attributes that could become sorting categories. They sort actual items in Boxes, Bottles, and Cans (p. 46), The Grocery Store (p. 48), and Clothing Sort (p. 51).

 **Choice Time**

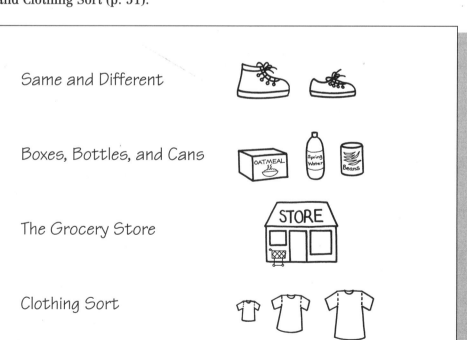

Same and Different

What Happens

Students choose a set of two similar objects with some distinct differences, for example, two sneakers—one black and one red. Working in pairs, they decide what's the same and what's different about the objects in their set. Students make some record of their observations so they can share their results with the group. Their work focuses on:

■ observing and describing attributes

■ identifying similarities and differences in attributes

Materials and Preparation

■ Gather 7–8 pairs of similar objects that are different in a clearly observable way (e.g., a wooden block and a plastic block, two different books, a cereal box and a tissue box). Store each pair in a resealable bag or a small box, labeled with a word and picture to show its contents.

■ Duplicate Student Sheet 1, Same and Different (p. 113), 1 per pair.

■ Have chart paper or board space available for recording students' ideas.

Activity

Introduce this activity by showing students one pair of similar objects.

I have two things in this box that you're going to look at very carefully. They're both sneakers. They are the *same* in some ways and *different* in some ways. To start, let's think about how these two things are the same. Talk with the person sitting next to you about your ideas.

After a few minutes, ask students to share their observations as you record their ideas on the board or chart paper. Divide the writing area in half, with one column for similarities and one for differences. Encourage students to be as specific as possible. When a list of similarities has been generated, ask students to describe how the items are different.

There are other sets of objects for you to look at during Choice Time. You and a partner choose one set. Describe both items in your set and think about ways that they are the same and ways that they are different. You can record your observations on this sheet [hold up a copy of Student Sheet 1, Same and Different].

Note: You may want to make the recording of their ideas optional. However, it's important for even the youngest students to have opportunities to make records of their work. There need not be an emphasis on recording in *words,* as few kindergartners will be capable of or interested in making a complete record this way. Instead, the emphasis should be on recording information in any way that makes sense to the student. Many kindergartners will make pictorial records, with some attempts at writing using invented spelling. Any such efforts give students valuable experience with recording their ideas.

Observing the Students

Consider the following as you observe pairs at work on the activity Same and Different.

- Do students understand the concepts of *same* and *different?*
- For each pair of objects, are students able to identify attributes that are the same and attributes that are different?
- Are students able to verbalize their ideas about like and unlike attributes?

Variations

- Students can put together their own pairs of objects to be compared. Remind them that the items in each set should be part of the same group (things to write with, kinds of hats, and so on), but should be different from each other in some easy-to-see way.
- Bring in photographs of familiar animals. Choose two at a time, and as a whole group make a list of how these two are the same and how they are different.

Sneakers

Same	Different
laces	color
rubber bottom	high/low top
stripes	old/new
has white	number of lace holes

Boxes, Bottles, and Cans

What Happens

Pairs of students choose a set of containers and sort these into two groups based on one attribute—that is, one group has the identified attribute (such as WHITE), and the other group does not (NOT WHITE). Students then sort the same objects in at least one other way. Their work focuses on:

■ grouping objects according to a shared attribute

■ using NOT as a category for organizing information

■ sorting a set of objects in more than one way

■ explaining the reasons for grouping objects in a given way

Materials and Preparation

■ Gather the three types of containers you have been collecting: small boxes, plastic bottles, and cans. (Boxes and bottles should be empty, but cans are better unopened to avoid dealing with sharp edges.)

■ Arrange the containers in sets of 8–10 boxes, 8–10 bottles, and 8–10 cans. (If you have extras, make additional sets.) The items within a set should be varied to allow for sorting in different ways. For example, a set of plastic bottles could include some clear and some colored, some round and some flatter in shape, some with caps and some without.

■ Store each set of containers in a larger box.

Activity

Point out the sets of boxes, bottles, and cans you have prepared. If students have contributed to these sets, acknowledge their help.

We've been collecting lots of different containers to use during math time. I put each kind of container in a separate box. That's one way that these things can be sorted: *[point to each set in turn]* **boxes, bottles, and cans.**

Today during Choice Time, you and a partner can choose one of these sets to work with. You'll be thinking about what's the *same* and what's *different* about the things in that set. For example, let's look at this set of plastic bottles. Who has an idea about which bottles might go together in a group?

Spread out the bottles so that students can see them all and take suggestions for ways they might be grouped. Try one or two ideas for sorting based on students' suggestions.

If no one suggests it, propose one sort with a NOT group.

When I sort the bottles this time, I'm going to make two groups. I'll put all the white bottles in one group, and the rest of the bottles in another group. So this is the group of WHITE bottles, and this is the group of NOT WHITE bottles.

Who can sort the bottles into two more groups, using NOT as one of the groups?

Explain to students that they can work with a partner on this activity. After sorting one set of objects in at least two ways, they may move on to a new Choice Time activity or sort a different set of containers.

Observing the Students

Consider the following as you watch student pairs at work on Boxes, Bottles, and Cans.

- Are students able to sort the objects into two groups, one being a NOT group?
- Do students sort with more than two groups? With more than two groups, students are likely to have objects that belong in more than one of their groups, such as WHITE BOTTLES and BOTTLES WITH LIDS. Observe how or if students address this issue.
- Can students verbalize their reasons for grouping objects together?

The Grocery Store

What Happens

Empty grocery containers are collected for use in a class grocery store. As a whole group, students discuss how the groceries in their store might be organized. A small group of students takes responsibility for arranging the groceries and making labels for the sections of the store. As a Choice Time activity for the rest of the class, students may shop and restock the shelves, take inventory, or work with money. Their work focuses on:

■ organizing objects according to similar attributes

■ thinking about why store items are organized as they are

Materials and Preparation

■ If possible, arrange a field trip to a grocery store to kick off the activity. If there are enough adult chaperones, take small groups of students to explore different sections of the store to see how the merchandise is organized.

■ Designate a small area in the classroom for the grocery store. If you have a dramatic play area or a house corner, consider using this for the store for the remainder of this unit.

■ Gather all the grocery items you have been collecting, including any that students have brought from home. As students complete the Boxes, Bottles, and Cans activity, these items can be added to the class store.

■ Make available index cards or small slips of paper for labeling grocery store shelves.

■ Have chart paper or board space available for recording students' ideas.

Activity

This activity has three parts:

■ planning how to organize the store (whole group)

■ setting up the store in the classroom (small groups)

■ using the store (individuals, pairs, and small groups)

Start with a whole-group discussion and planning session.

How many of you have been to a grocery store? Think for a minute about how the people who work in the store arrange things so they're easy to find. For example, if you want to buy some cereal for breakfast, where would you look? What if you wanted to buy some frozen juice bars for snack?

How is the food organized in a grocery store? Why does this make sense?

Would it make sense to organize the things in a grocery store by color or by size? Why or why not?

Planning the Store Explain that a small group of students is going to help set up a class grocery store using the empty boxes, cans, and other items that have been collected. As students generate a list of ideas about how the store might be organized, record the ideas on chart paper for future reference. Encourage students to explain their plans.

Observing the Students

Consider the following as you listen to students' plans for the class grocery store.

- Do students discuss other ways of organizing the store besides putting identical foods together?
- Are students able to explain why they think their organization makes sense?

Setting Up the Store Many students will probably be interested in being part of the setup crew, but this doesn't work well as a whole-group activity. Reassure students that everyone will have an opportunity to visit and work in the store once it has been set up.

Choose groups of three or four students for the setup. Encourage them to use the ideas the class generated and to talk about how they will sort and organize the items before they begin the actual work. Provide index cards or slips of paper for shelf labels, and offer help with writing words.

Using the Store This activity can be as simple or elaborate as you choose. You may want to suggest specific roles that students can fill when using the store during Choice Time. For example, one student might check out the groceries, while one or two other students shop. Another one or two could restock the shelves, returning items that have been purchased previously to their appropriate places.

On some days, students can take inventory to find out how many of each type of item they have in the store.

You might also introduce money into the store experience. A small group of students could take a single shelf or a single type of product and decide the price of each item. Dot stickers marked with prices could be placed on the groceries. Keep costs between 1¢ and 5¢. Then after students shop, they can figure out how much their groceries cost.

Clothing Sort

What Happens

Students sort clothing items in a variety of ways, according to size, type, color, and so on. This activity begins in the whole class with each student taking charge of one article of clothing. After discussing different ways to group the clothing, the class sorts according to one of these suggestions. During Choice Time, small groups of students find other ways to sort the clothing. Students' work focuses on:

- sorting according to the presence or absence of one attribute
- sorting by various attributes, including use or function

Materials and Preparation

- Collect sets of clothing in three distinct sizes: one set for an infant or toddler, one for a kindergartner, and one for an adult. A set of clothing might include shirt, pants, socks, shoes, hat, a coat or sweater, and mittens or gloves. There should be at least one item of clothing per student.
- Store clothing in a large box or plastic bag.

Activity

Distribute one article of clothing to each student. They take turns holding up the clothing and telling what each item is.

Each of you has one piece of clothing from our box [or bag]. Who has an idea about how we might group or organize these clothes? Is there anything the same about some of these clothes?

After students suggest several ways that they might sort the clothing into groups, choose one idea to try out with the whole class.

Then explain that during Choice Time, students can gather in groups of three or four to sort the same clothes in different ways. Kindergartners are likely to sort by color, by size, by type or function (all gloves or all shoes, for example), and by material, among other things.

Consider the following as you watch groups of students at work on Clothing Sort.

- How do students sort the clothing? Do they use size or function as a way of sorting?
- How do students describe the groups they have made? Can they explain their reasons for creating these groups?
- Are students able to sort the items in more than one way?

When most students have sorted the clothing during Choice Time, you might ask one group to sort the clothes according to the size of the person who would wear them and then arrange the outfits on the floor in the meeting area. This not only engages students in a sorting activity, but also allows them to see relative size as they compare the clothes in each set.

Choosing Categories

Many kindergarten classrooms use graphs as a way of collecting information about students. Familiar subjects for graphs include these:

- How old are you?
- What kind of pet do you have?
- What's your favorite color?
- How many people are in your family?

These questions represent two types of information to be collected: *categorical* data, or data that can be sorted according to attributes; and *numerical* data, or data that can be ordered in a particular way. The pet and favorite color questions will yield categorical data, whereas the number of people in a family and students' ages are numerical data.

In the activity What Did You Eat for Lunch? students collect categorical data about the favorite part of lunch for everyone in the class. They are then asked to think about the different ways these foods can be grouped. Students decide on categories that make sense to them based on the real data they have collected. Because a permanent representation of the data is not made until the end of the activity, students are able to try out different ways of sorting their favorite lunch foods.

The choosing of categories by the students themselves is a key element in representing categorical data. Too often in the primary classroom, data collection and representation are tied to predetermined categories. The categories are defined, usually by the teacher, before the data are collected, and students are limited to a few choices. While this simplifies the task, it also precludes the richness and diversity that can result when students have the chance to consider how and why certain data go together. For example, in the **Dialogue Box,** But My Peach Was Sweet (p. 55), one kindergartner makes a distinction between *sweet* desserts (cookies, brownies) and *fruit* desserts (apples, grapes). While this organization is clear and understandable to that student, it is confusing to a classmate who points out that his peach was also sweet.

Involving students in making decisions about how things go together brings them into some of the most important aspects of data collection. While we as teachers may want to define categories in order to make a task easier to understand, what is understandable to us may be puzzling to someone else. Only through sorting the actual data they have collected can students arrive at categories that have meaning for them. In the process, even the youngest students encounter an important idea in data analysis: that different ways of organizing data make different aspects of the data more obvious and salient. When students are allowed and encouraged to be involved in all aspects of data collection and analysis, the process becomes a rich, active experience rather than a passive exercise of responding to a predetermined graph.

Any investigation of data does not end with the creation of a graph or other representation. In fact, much of the real work begins *after* the data have been organized and represented. Graphs and other representations are vehicles for communication. Thinking about what they communicate is an activity that even young students can and should experience.

One type of data analysis that is generally obvious to students is a *quantitative* approach. Observations such as "Six people like pizza" or "Four more people chose pizza than chose peanut butter" give particular numeric information about a graph.

Qualitative observations can give different information about the same data. Statements such as "A lot more people liked sweet desserts than liked fruit desserts" or "Most people chose either pizza or dessert as the favorite part of their lunch" capture important information about the data without using exact numbers.

Each time a graph or representation is created, it is important to engage students in some discussion of the information it communicates. The following questions can help promote data analysis in classroom discussions:

■ What do you think this graph (or representation) is about?

■ What does this graph tell us?

■ What do you notice about this graph? What's interesting about it?

■ What can you say about the favorite part of our lunch by looking at this graph?

■ If we asked the same question in another classroom, collected the data, and made a graph, do you think the graph would look the same as this one or different?

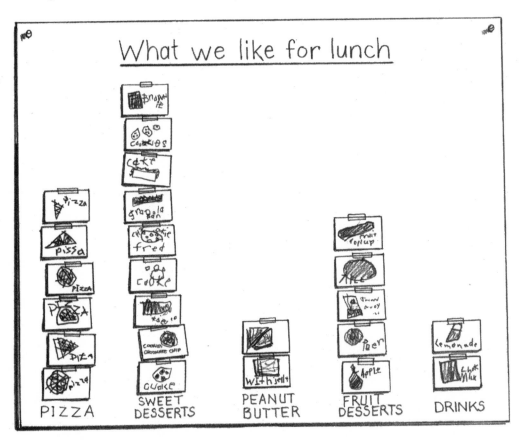

D I A L O G U E   B O X

But My Peach Was Sweet

In this discussion, students are talking about ways of organizing their favorite lunch foods. Although the categories that students suggest leave many possibilities for overlapping, the teacher is careful not to impose groupings, instead allowing students to make their own decisions about how the lunch data go together.

Maddy: I think the pizza people should all be together. That's me and Justine and Luke.

Ida: Some people liked the same things, like cookies. We should be in a group, too.

Jacob: I like my dessert the best, and today it was a brownie. So I could go in the cookie group, too.

Can you say why you think your brownie goes with the cookie group?

Jacob: Well, it's sort of like a cookie. Sometimes I have cookies for dessert too.

Is there a way to describe foods like cookies and brownies?

Kadim: We could say sweet things.

Ravi: They're all things you have for dessert.

Shanique: And they're things I like! We could say it's things you like.

Renata: I think we should call it dessert.

I've heard a few suggestions for types of groups. Maddy suggested the PIZZA group and a couple of people suggested a DESSERT group.

Let's start some groups. The people who think they belong in the PIZZA group, sit over here next to the bookshelf. The people who think they belong in the DESSERT group, come sit by the game shelf.

Kadim: I think we should have a sweet group, too.

Henry: I had a peach as my favorite thing, but it's not the same kind of dessert as cookies.

Felipe: I think I go with Henry. I have an apple and that's fruit.

Renata: We should have a *fruit dessert* group and a *sweet dessert* group.

Henry: But my peach was sweet.

So which group would your peach go in?

Henry: A peach is more like an apple than it's like a cookie, so I'll go in the fruit desserts.

Kadim, you had the idea for a SWEET group. How does this sound to you?

Kadim: Well, I had peanut butter and fluff as my favorite and it's sort of sweet, but I think I go with Thomas. He has peanut butter too.

You have lots of interesting ideas about how things go together. Let's add the FRUIT DESSERT group and the PEANUT BUTTER group. Then we can see which people go where, and who is left.

Our Favorite Lunch Foods

pizza	popcorn	chocolate milk	fruit chews
pizza	peach	p. b. & jelly sandwich	juice box
juice box	pizza	cookies	granola bar
brownie	strawberries	fruit roll-up	apple
chips	macaroni & cheese	cookie	cake
popcorn	string cheese	p. b. & fluff sandwich	lemonade

INVESTIGATION 3

Collecting Data About Our Class

Focus Time

Yes/No Surveys (p. 58)

The Attendance routine is revisited as an introduction to the yes/no type of survey. Students then go through the steps of taking their own simple survey with a question that can be answered yes or no. They choose a question to ask their classmates, plan how to collect and keep track of responses to their question, and make observations about the data they collected.

Choice Time

Yes/No Surveys (p. 66)

Students continue to conduct their own surveys. When they are done, they present the results to their classmates.

Continuing from Investigations 1 and 2

Boxes, Bottles, and Cans (p. 46)

The Grocery Store (p. 48)

Pattern Block Grab (p. 30)

Mathematical Emphasis

- Composing survey questions
- Gathering and recording data
- Counting the items in different groups
- Comparing the sizes of different groups
- Making sense of data representations
- Sorting by like attributes into two groups
- Describing categories for a sort

Teacher Support

Teacher Notes

Choosing Yes/No Survey Questions (p. 68)

Examining Young Students' Data Representations (p. 69)

Dialogue Boxes

Are You Here Today? (p. 72)

What's Your Favorite Ice Cream? (p. 73)

Will All Our Seeds Germinate? (p. 74)

What to Plan Ahead of Time

Focus Time Materials

Yes/No Surveys

- Clothespins: 1 per student, labeled on both sides with the student's name (see p. 58)
- Survey board made from poster board or sturdy cardboard cut to about 8 by 36 inches (see p. 58 for further details)
- Chart paper
- Class list: 1–2 per student (includes supply for Choice Time)
- Student Sheet 2, Yes/No Survey Chart (p. 114): 1–2 per student (includes supply for Choice Time)
- Unlined paper: 1–2 sheets per student
- Clipboards: 1 per student, optional (can be handmade by attaching a sheet of paper to a book or stiff cardboard with a large paper clip, clothespin, or binder clip)

Choice Time Materials

Yes/No Surveys

- Class lists, paper, copies of Student Sheet 2, and optional clipboards from Focus Time

Boxes, Bottles, and Cans

- Sets of boxes, empty plastic bottles, and unopened cans, stored in boxes, from Investigation 2

The Grocery Store

- Class store as set up in Investigation 2

Pattern Block Grab

- Pattern blocks: 1 bucket per 4–6 students
- Unlined paper: 1 sheet per student
- Crayons or markers

Focus Time

Yes/No Surveys

What Happens

In this introduction to simple surveys (using questions that can be answered yes or no), students first collect and discuss attendance data, using a survey board and "name pins." Students then choose their own yes/no questions and take their own surveys. Their work focuses on:

- composing a yes/no survey question
- collecting data
- representing the data
- counting and comparing the numbers in different groups

Materials and Preparation

- If you do not already have "name pins" prepared as suggested in *Mathematical Thinking in Kindergarten,* make a set by printing each student's name in permanent marker on both sides of a clothespin. Be sure the name is right side up whether the clip is to the right or to the left.

- Make a survey board from poster board or sturdy cardboard, 8 inches across and about 36 inches tall (depending on your class size). Divide the board into three sections. Draw a vertical line down the center of the bottom two sections only.

  The top section has no vertical line dividing it; the survey question is taped in this space.

  In the section below the question, write the survey responses YES and NO.

  Divide the bottom section into rows about 1 inch deep, 1 row for each student in your class. This is where their name pins will be clipped.

  On a sheet of paper cut to fit in the top section of the survey board, write the question *Are you here today?* Lightly tape the question onto the board.

- Duplicate copies of your class list, 1–2 per student, and Student Sheet 2, Yes/No Survey Chart (p. 114), 2–3 per student (includes supply for Choice Time).

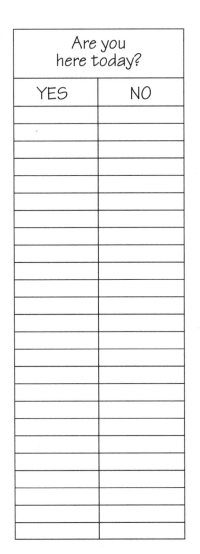

Are you here today?	
YES	NO

Are You Here Today?

Note: Some teachers will have already been using name pins and survey boards for the Attendance and Today's Question routines (as discussed in the section About Classroom Routines, pp. 93–103). If that is the case, this activity can be just a brief reminder of their use while you introduce or review the yes/no survey format.

Distribute the name pins or lay them out so that students can find their own. Explain that these are data collection tools—tools they can use to survey or collect information about their class. Also present the survey board you have prepared.

This is our survey board. It's a place for us to collect information about our class using your name pins. Today the question on the survey board is about attendance. The question says, *Are you here today*?

If you have done the classroom attendance routine earlier today, explain that this will show them a new way to collect the same information. Demonstrate how to clip the pins onto the sides of the board, pointing out that each space on the board is for one pin.

Students come up one or two at a time to clip their pins on the board. When everyone has responded, clip the name pins of the absent students to the No side of the board. Then ask students what they can tell from the data they have collected.

How would you explain to a guest in our classroom what this survey is about?

Asking students to explain a survey encourages them to interpret the information that is being collected. It is easy for students to focus on just the process of collecting data and to lose sight of the meaning of the data. If students are unsure what the survey or graph is about, reread the question on the survey board to remind them.

What do you notice about this survey?

Students' responses to this question can give you some insights into what they understand about the "graph" they have created on the survey board and what aspects of the graph or data are important to them. Some students might comment on the number of people who are present and the number who are absent. Some might make comparative statements such as, "More people are here today," or "A lot more people are here than are absent." Some students might notice that the number of empty spaces on the Yes side of the graph is equal to the number of people who are absent.

Some students might make observations that have little or nothing to do with the data, for example, "The words *yes* and *no* are red," or "Some kids' names are bigger than others." Accept all observations, including those that are unrelated to the data. Students will learn more about looking at data through repeated discussions about the different data sets they collect.

If students do not comment on the specific number of people who are present and absent, ask them to do so.

Using this graph, is there a way to figure out how many from our class are in school today? . . . How can we double-check this information?

To double-check, students will likely suggest counting the number of people present in the meeting area. Do this by going around the circle as students count off. Record this information on chart paper or the board. Then ask about the number of people who are *not* in school and record that information as well.

If we counted all the name pins on this graph, how many do you think there would be?

As students offer their ideas, ask them to explain their thinking. Listen for explanations that suggest students are making a one-to-one correspondence between the total number of students in the class and the total number of name pins. Record this information as well.

There are 19 kids in school today.

There are 6 kids not in school today.

There are 25 kids in our class.

Today we collected some data about who is here and who is not here. Can you think of any reasons why that might be important information? Why might we need to use those data?

Thinking about how graphs can be useful to us is an important aspect of collecting and analyzing data.

Collecting attendance data using name pins and the survey board is an activity that can be repeated many times with students; if you are not already doing so, consider taking this approach to vary your usual attendance routine. See the **Dialogue Box,** Are You Here Today?, for the discussion that resulted in one class after three days of using the survey board for attendance.

Choosing Survey Questions

When we first used our survey boards and name pins, we found out some information about who was in school and who was absent. I asked a question, and the answer to that question was either *yes* or *no.* That was like taking a class survey.

For the next few days, you will have a chance to do more surveys, asking questions and collecting information from the people in our classroom. Just like the attendance question, the people you ask should be able to answer your question by saying either yes or no.

Offer students a few examples of yes/no questions and then ask for their ideas for questions. While using only yes/no questions may seem somewhat constrained, it is a good way for students to begin looking at survey results as it gives them only two categories of data to compare. Of course, there will be times when what seems to be a yes/no question will elicit a response of "maybe" or "sometimes." See the **Teacher Note,** Choosing Yes/No Survey Questions (p. 68), for guidelines on selecting questions and handling "maybe" responses.

If your students have been doing the classroom routine Today's Question on a regular basis (see p. 100), they will be familiar with this type of question. Otherwise, you may need to help them shape their questions. The **Dialogue Box,** What's Your Favorite Ice Cream? (p. 73), illustrates how one teacher helped her students formulate suitable questions.

On chart paper or the board, make a list of the questions students generate. If this is your class's first experience with this type of question, consider narrowing down the possible survey questions to three or four; students can then select one of these to investigate.

Then introduce the tools students might use for collecting data: clipboards (if available), your class list, and paper for recording the data, including both unlined paper and copies of Student Sheet 2, Yes/No Survey Chart. Depending on your students' prior experience with surveys, talk with them about how they could use each of these tools.

Although Student Sheet 2 is a useful tool for collecting data, it's a good idea to encourage students to create and organize their own data collection sheets as well. Be sure to point out the completely blank paper they could use, and talk with them about the important parts of a data collection sheet.

When we did our attendance survey, we used a survey board and name pins to collect the data. You won't be able to use those tools when you take your own surveys because you'll all be working on different ideas at the same time. That means you'll have to come up with your own way to collect your data. What are some of the things you'll need to include on your paper?

As necessary, refer students to the attendance survey done with name pins. The key elements they should identify are the survey question, the possible answers to the question (*yes* and *no*), and a place to keep track of the data.

Students should make their own decisions about what format to use and what to include on their chart. Make clear that Student Sheet 2 is just one option. Observing how students organize their work can give you valuable insights into their understanding of the process of taking surveys. In addition, the class will have the chance to look at and discuss a variety of approaches to organizing and representing data. For some examples of the variation in kindergarten work, see the **Teacher Note**, Examining Young Students' Data Representations (p. 69).

Activity

Collecting Survey Data

Some students may want to work with a partner on this activity. Each student or pair should choose a survey question and the materials they will use. Before they begin to collect the data, their question should be written at the top of their survey chart (provide assistance as needed).

Once you have written down your question and organized your sheet so you know where you will write down the information people are telling you, you will be ready to ask people your survey question.

If your students have little or no experience with surveys, you might ask a few of them to role-play asking a survey question to a classmate.

Whether or not to begin taking surveys during your whole-group meeting time depends on the size of your class and how your day is organized. You may prefer that students only choose a question and prepare their data collection sheets at this time, leaving data collection for Choice Time when you can limit the activity to six or eight students at a time.

As students complete their surveys, whether during Focus Time or Choice Time, spend a few minutes talking with them individually about their data. Just as you did with the class attendance survey, ask students to count the Yes and No responses and write the results on their paper. Also help students think about what their survey means.

What was your survey about? . . . What did you find out about [your question]?

As clusters of students finish their surveys, invite them to share their results during a whole-group meeting. If students do not finish a survey during Focus Time, be sure they understand that they will have a chance to do so during Choice Time. Surveys can even be an ongoing Choice Time activity after your class work with this unit has ended.

Keep in mind that for this initial experience with data collection, accuracy and consistency will not be of great concern to most students. Refer to the **Teacher Note,** Examining Young Students' Data Representations (p. 69), for a discussion of how this improves with experience.

Observing the Students

Consider the following as you watch students preparing their surveys, collecting their data, and analyzing their results.

■ Were students able to choose a question that can be answered by only yes or no?

■ How do students organize their survey charts?

■ How do students record people's responses?

■ Do students have or want a system for keeping track of whom they have surveyed so far?

■ Are students able to count up the number of responses for each category of data?

■ Are students able to explain their survey results with such statements as "Most people in our class don't like rain" or "More people have pockets than don't have pockets today"?

Focus Time Follow-Up

 **Choice Time**

Four Choices During Choice Time, students continue the work of conducting their own yes/no surveys in the classroom. In addition, they may continue their work on two activities from Investigation 2: Boxes, Bottles, and Cans (p. 46) and The Grocery Store (p. 48). A good fourth choice would be Pattern Block Grab (p. 30), a data sorting activity from Investigation 1.

Yes/No Surveys

What Happens

Students continue the work with surveys they began in Focus Time. When they finish a survey, they have a conversation with the teacher about it before presenting the results to their classmates. Their work focuses on:

- composing yes/no survey questions
- collecting and recording data
- explaining and interpreting results of surveys
- presenting data to others

Materials and Preparation

- Provide copies of the class list and Student Sheet 2, Yes/No Survey Chart, as well as a supply of unlined paper.
- If you have clipboards, continue to make these available.

Activity

During Choice Time, students may be finishing surveys they began in Focus Time or starting on new ones. In either case, plan to limit data collection to six or eight students at a time. As needed, remind students of the following:

- They may want to work with a partner.
- Their survey question should be written at the top of their survey chart before they begin to collect data.
- When they have finished collecting data, they find the total number of responses for each category.
- They meet with you to talk about their results before putting their survey away.

Remind students that class lists are available. As they do more and more data collection on their own, they will begin to regard the class list as a helpful tool for keeping track of the people they have interviewed.

Observing the Students

Consider the following as you meet with students about the results of their yes/no surveys.

- How do students record the responses to their survey?
- Do students have or want a system for keeping track of whom they have surveyed and whom they have not yet surveyed?
- Are students able to count the number of responses for each category of data?
- Are students able to explain their survey results with such statements as "Most people in our class like carrots" or "More people have a pet than don't have a pet"?

If your students have had a lot of experience with data during the kindergarten year, ask them to consider some of the following:

How do you know if everyone in the class has answered your survey?

Compare the number of responses in each category. Which has more? How many more?

If you were to ask your question in a different kindergarten class, do you think you would get the same number of yeses and nos? Why or why not?

From time to time, plan a whole-group meeting when students can share their survey results.

During this data investigation, students work primarily with yes/no survey questions. Working with only two categories of data can help students see the part-whole relationship between the numbers for each response and the total number of students in the class.

We recommend that you involve students in brainstorming their own questions; however, coming up with workable yes/no survey questions can be quite difficult for kindergartners—and surprisingly tricky for adults. As you generate yes/no questions, consider the following possible formats:

Can you . . .

> hop on one foot?
>
> tie your shoes?

Are you . . .

> 6 years old?
>
> the oldest child in your family?

Do you have . . .

> a younger brother or sister?
>
> a pet?
>
> brown eyes?

Are you wearing . . .

> clothing with pockets?
>
> a shirt with a collar?
>
> the color red?

Be aware that sensitive issues may be raised by questions involving material possessions or opportunities that all students do not have.

Depending on the experience of your students and their facility with inventing suitable questions, you may want to pose several survey questions and ask students to select one.

As you and your students think of yes/no questions, you will probably discover that there are some questions for which yes and no are the only logical responses (Are you 5 years old? Do you have a pet?), and other questions for which there are additional possible responses such as *maybe, sometimes,* or *I'm not sure.* Consider for example, these questions:

Do you think it will rain today?

Do you like to play outside?

Do you eat lunch at school?

Even a straightforward question such as "Do you like carrots?" elicited responses other than yes and no in one class. For some students, the answer depended on whether the carrots were cooked or raw, so their response was "sometimes." Our experience has been that students are able to deal with such responses, often inventing a way to record and keep track of them. We have also noticed that after several experiences with surveys, many students begin to plan for alternative responses to their survey questions.

Whether students think up their own questions or work with questions that you provide, we recommend that they make their own decisions about the potential responses to those questions. The **Dialogue Box,** Will All Our Seeds Germinate? (p. 74), offers an example of how one group of kindergarten students and their teacher grappled with this issue.

Examining Young Students' Data Representations

When kindergarten students have the opportunity to participate actively in data collection, they are likely to choose questions and topics that have meaning and relevance to their own lives. But even with this involvement, it takes time for young students to adopt many of the protocols of data collection and representation, such as creating a logical way to keep track of all the pieces of data they collect and representing the information in an organized way.

When students are first involved in collecting data on their own, it is important to allow them to proceed in a way that makes sense to them. We have found that most kindergarten students are engaged first by the process of collecting data—preparing the survey sheet, interviewing classmates, and recording responses. Data collection starts as a primarily social experience for them, and issues such as being sure to collect data from every student in the class, or comparing results with someone who asked the same question, are not of much concern. Many teachers have found that, as students gain experience, they begin to see the need for accuracy and consistency in data collection. As this happens, students begin to make better use of tools and strategies that improve accuracy in both collecting and representing the data.

The five examples that follow demonstrate how these kindergartners kept track of the data they were collecting for their yes/no surveys.

Tiana's survey

Tiana chose her question, "Do you have a baby brother or sister?" because of the birth of a new sibling in her family. As she collected data from her classmates, she recorded the name of each person and "yes" or "no" to indicate that person's response. Tiana is beginning to understand the need to record her respondents and the information she collects from them, although she has not yet developed a systematic way of keeping track of whom she has asked and whom she still needs to ask.

Continued on next page

"This is a graph about Do You Have a Pet? The numbers next to yes tell how many."

YES — NO
YESS — NO
YESS — NO
— NO
YESS — NO
YESS — NO
YESS
YESS
YESS — N O

Oscar's survey

"Do you like invented spelling?"

P 8 < 6 5 4 3 2 1

ALETA
YES
KYLIE
TIANA
IDA — MIYUKI
HENRY — THOMAS — CHARLOTTE
JUSTINE — GABRIELA — CARLO
LUKE
TARIK — JE NIQ SHA

YES   NO   BE MA

Gabriela's survey

Oscar's question (Do you have a pet?) interested him because he had just added two hamsters to his pet collection, which already included a cat and a dog. Oscar has grouped like responses and recorded his data in a way that enables him to compare the two groups directly (although it looks as if he may have stopped collecting data when he ran out of space). Oscar, like Tiana, has yet to think of an effective way to keep track of who still hasn't been interviewed.

Gabriela's representation shows a great deal of information and reflects a purposeful use of data collection. Gabriela was interested in finding out how many of her classmates liked invented spelling, a practice that she herself was not fond of. She hoped that if she could show that enough of her classmates felt as she did, invented spelling would no longer be used in her classroom. Gabriela arranged her data in a relatively traditional bar graph. She used 1-inch graph paper to organize the information into three columns for the categories Yes, No, and Maybe ["MABE"]. However, the data cannot be compared directly across the columns because some responses have been crossed out. Like Tiana and Oscar, Gabriela did not collect data from every student in the class, but she does show evidence of understanding the importance of recording and organizing the data she has collected.

Continued on next page

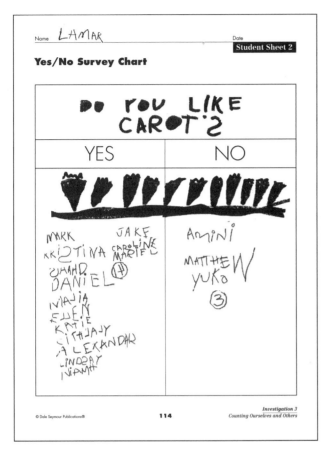

Lamar's survey

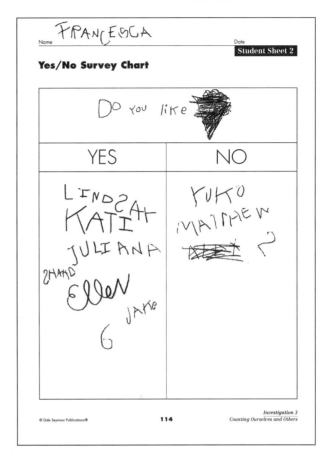

Francesca's survey

In another class, the teacher decided to use Student Sheet 2 for collecting data for the yes/no survey questions. The format was familiar since the students had been using it as part of the classroom routine, Today's Question. The teacher focused this data collection project on the vegetable garden that the class was planting. Lamar and Francesca each collected data about whether students liked carrots. They were able to record responses in the appropriate sections and to count the total number of people in each category. It was interesting to the teacher that few students seemed concerned about whether they had polled everyone in the class (although Lamar came close, surveying 17 out of 20), or about the fact that some students (like Lamar and Francesca) asked the same question and got different results. Knowing there would be many

more opportunities to talk about data collection, the teacher made a plan to visit these points in whole-class discussions after the next survey.

Collecting, recording, and representing data are important aspects of every experience with data. While we can offer students tools and strategies for doing each of these things, we cannot assume that our offerings are useful until the students have had numerous experiences with the process of data collection. It is only with these experiences, guided by the teacher, that students will consider why it's important to collect data from everyone or to organize data so that the results can be easily understood. And only when students work with these issues themselves will they find practical and meaningful ways to use the tools and strategies they are offered.

Are You Here Today?

After introducing the use of name pins and a survey board for taking attendance, this teacher continues using it on subsequent days for the attendance routine. On the third day, the teacher notices that students are describing the data in a variety of ways. They are also using the representation to make comparisons between the two groups of data, and they are noticing how the data have changed over time.

For this discussion, the students can see 21 pins clipped on the Yes side and 4 on the No side of the survey board. The teacher begins the discussion by asking students to interpret the attendance graph.

Who can tell us something that they notice about our attendance graph today?

Miyuki: There's more people who are here than who are not here today.

Maddy: It's different.

Different?

Maddy: Different from yesterday. Yesterday there were 5 kids on the No side, but Ravi is back so now he's on the Yes side.

Luke: And the number changed. It went up like 20 and then 21. And that number *[pointing to the No side]* went down.

So you noticed how the data have changed from yesterday to today. And yes, Ravi is back in school today. Welcome back, Ravi.

Kylie: I notice there's four people who're not here and *[counting the name pins on the Yes side]* 1, 2, 3, . . . 21 people who are here today.

Tess: The Yes side has a lot more pins on it than the No side.

What do you suppose that means?

Tess: That there are a lot of people in school today?

Shanique: Hey, there's four people who aren't here, and there's four empty spaces down there *[pointing to the bottom of the Yes side]*.

Kylie and Shanique both noticed that four people are not here today, but they were looking at different parts of the survey board. Kylie counted the four name pins on the No side of the board, and Shanique counted the four empty spaces on the Yes side. Shanique, how do you know that four people are absent by looking at the Yes side?

Shanique: Because when everyone is here, there's no empty spaces.

Kylie: And see, if you keep counting from here *[pointing to the last name pin on the Yes side]*, that's 21, and then you go *[keeping track on her fingers]* 22, 23, 24, 25—that's four!

So you can find the same information in different places on this survey board. Now, Maddy noticed that today's data are different from yesterday's data. Do you think the data will change tomorrow?

Maddy: Well, maybe if Ida or Felipe or Jacob comes back. But I know Justine will be on the No side 'cause she's away on a trip and she's not coming back tomorrow.

Kylie counted 21 name pins on the Yes side of the survey board. Is there a way we could double-check that number to see if it is correct?

Tess: We could count off like we sometimes do.

OK, let's start on one side of our circle and count off. If our data are correct, how many of us should there be?

Students: 21!

What's Your Favorite Ice Cream?

This kindergarten class is brainstorming possible questions for yes/no surveys. Students are interested in thinking up their own survey questions, but finding questions that can be answered only by yes or no is a challenge for some of them. Wanting to accept students' ideas, the teacher helps out by asking questions to help them narrow the focus.

Tarik: I'm going to do the one you said about "Do you have a brother?" I have a brother and I *am* a brother!

Ayesha: Mine is going to be, "What's your favorite kind of ice cream?"

What are some of the answers you might get when you ask that question?

Ayesha: Chocolate, because it's my favorite. Maybe someone would like vanilla or chocolate chip.

Jacob: I like cookie dough. It's my favorite.

Alexa: And I like peppermint stick. Yum!

So, there are lots of different kinds of ice cream flavors that people like. For this survey, we're trying to ask a question that can be answered with either yes or no. Ayesha, can you think about how to change your ice cream question so that it can have a yes or no answer?

[Ayesha shakes her head no and shrugs her shoulders.]

Okay, I have a question for you, Ayesha. Do you like ice cream?

Ayesha: Yes!

Do you think other students in our class like ice cream?

Ayesha: *[laughing]* Yes!

Do you like chocolate ice cream?

Ayesha: Yes! It's my favorite.

Do you think other people like chocolate ice cream the best?

Ayesha: Well, maybe, I don't know.

Jacob: I know—you could ask people if they like ice cream. That could be the question because you could say "Yes, I like ice cream" or "No, I don't like ice cream."

Ayesha: Or I could ask them if they like chocolate ice cream, because I like chocolate ice cream, and that could be yes or no.

Will All Our Seeds Germinate?

One teacher decided to incorporate data collection and yes/no survey questions into a part of the science curriculum that the students especially enjoy. Each spring this class plants sunflower seeds, which are then transplanted to a local farm. In the fall, when the students return as first graders, they harvest the sunflowers for the seeds.

In this activity, the teacher is working with a group of six students. They are planning to survey the class about whether they think their sunflower seeds will germinate. The students become very involved in a discussion about the possible responses to the question "Will all our seeds germinate?"

Ravi: Well, maybe half will grow and half won't.

Kylie: I think more than half. I think just three won't germinate.

If we were going to make a survey question about our seeds, what would we need to do?

Xing-Qi: We first think about it.

Charlotte: We need lines on the paper and then you put down the words and then you write down *Yes, No,* and *I'm not sure.*

***Yes, No,* and *I'm not sure*—do these answers work for this question?**

Charlotte: You could say "*Yes* they will all grow," "*No* they won't," and "*I'm not sure* if they will." So they work.

Brendan: I think you could put *A lot, A little,* or *Not at all.*

Ravi: What if you say "I think half will germinate"? Then you should have *Yes, No, I'm not sure,* and *I think half will grow.*

Kylie: That's a good idea. We need a ruler to draw lines.

So, how should we set up the paper if we were going to make this a class survey question? Where should the lines be?

Kylie: Like this. *[She uses a ruler to show how she would draw vertical lines on the paper to divide it into four response columns.]*

Charlotte: But my name is too long to go in that space. When I write it, it might bump into the next space. It should be bigger.

Kylie: We could leave out *I'm not sure.* It's like *No.*

Are they the same thing?

Carlo: *No* means that's your answer. It's different from *I'm not sure* because *I'm not sure* means you aren't sure.

Xing-Qi: *I'm not sure* and *Half will grow* is the same.

Carlo: No, *half will grow* means I think half the seeds will grow. That's not like *I'm not sure.*

Brendan: I think if we don't put *I'm not sure,* then Henry will pick something else. He always picks *I'm not sure.*

Kylie: We could not use *I'm not sure* but instead use *Maybe.*

Ravi: If we just put *Yes* and *No,* we can just put the line in the middle.

Charlotte: But what if you're not sure?

At first I thought we would all work on the same kind of chart, but should we each make a different one?

Kylie: Do *Maybe.*

Is *Maybe* the same thing as *I'm not sure?*

Charlotte: No.

Xing-Qi: Both mean *I'm not sure.*

Brendan: Yeah, that's right.

I'm going to get more paper so that you each can design your own survey chart.

Charlotte: But *Maybe* is not the same.

Since each of you is going to design your own survey, you can choose to include *I'm not sure* as one of your choices, Charlotte.

After this discussion, the students decided for themselves how many responses to allow for. Some of their survey charts are shown below.

Who's Here? Who's Not?

Focus Time

Who's Here? Who's Not? (p. 78)

Students consider a familiar attendance problem from a new angle: Given the total number of students in our class and the number who are absent today, how many are here today? They build models and make representations of the data in order to show how they tackled the problem. During Choice Time, they continue to work on activities from previous investigations.

Choice Time

Continuing from Investigations 2 and 3

Yes/No Surveys (p. 66)

The Grocery Store (p. 48)

Mathematical Emphasis

- Solving a mathematical problem based on data
- Building a model or making a representation to explain a problem-solving strategy.
- Counting and comparing sets of objects or people

Teacher Support

Teacher Notes

From the Classroom: How Many Are Here Today? (p. 82)

Understanding Students' Work (p. 84)

25 in our class
4 absent
How many are here?

What to Plan Ahead of Time

Focus Time Materials

Who's Here? Who's Not?

- Art materials such as dot stickers, 1-inch squares of colored paper, crayons, markers, colored pencils, glue sticks
- Interlocking cubes, buttons, counters of various kinds
- Large drawing paper: 1 sheet per student

Choice Time Materials

Yes/No Surveys

- Copies of the class list and Student Sheet 2, Yes/No Survey Chart, plus a supply of unlined paper, from Investigation 3
- Clipboards: 1 per student, optional

The Grocery Store

- Class store as set up in Investigation 2

Who's Here?
Who's Not?

What Happens

In a class discussion about the daily attendance data, the class makes a list of students who *are not* in school, then discusses ways of determining how many students *are* in school. They make a model or representation of these data in order to show and explain to someone else how they know the number of students in school today. Their work focuses on:

- counting as a way of collecting data
- keeping track of a count
- comparing quantities
- representing data

Materials and Preparation

- For students' representations of the data, provide a variety of small manipulatives (interlocking cubes, buttons, counters of various kinds) and art materials (dot stickers, 1-inch squares of colored paper, crayons, markers, colored pencils, glue sticks).
- Provide a sheet of drawing paper for each student.

Before You Begin

This Focus Time involves the comparison of two numbers—the number of students present in your class and the number absent—so you'll want to do the activity on a day when there isn't perfect attendance. It's also a good idea to repeat the activity at another time, when different students are absent, so that everyone gets a chance to do it.

Since the activity looks at attendance data for one specific day, it's important to finish all the work within that same day. Plan on a total of about one hour for students to work through the two Focus Time activities. If it's more convenient, you can break them up, doing the first activity early and the second one toward the end of the school day.

How Many Are Here Today?

Begin by reviewing your daily attendance routine and its purpose.

You know that every day we take attendance, and we let the office know who isn't here.

Today we're going to think about this as a mathematical problem. Let's start with the number of people in our class. When everyone is here, how many of us are in this room?

Students can decide whether to limit this count to themselves or to include adults present in the classroom. If you have saved students' representations of How Many Are We? in Investigation 1, you can use these to remind students of the total number in the class.

Ask students to help you name their classmates who are not in school today. List these names on the board or chart paper.

Not Here Today

Kadim

Tess

Maddy

Felipe

Here is the problem I would like you to think about today. We know that there are [25 students] in our class. Today, [4 students] are not here. The problem is this: How many students are here in class today?

Your job is to make a model, draw a picture, or use numbers to figure out this problem. You can use any materials in our classroom. Who has an idea for how you might figure out how many students are here today?

Ask for volunteers to share their strategies. Most likely some students will suggest, "We could just count everyone who is here." Acknowledge this idea as one way to solve the problem, and tell students that you are also interested in *other* ways of figuring out how many people are in the room. Show students the variety of materials available to them, including both counters and art supplies.

The **Teacher Note,** From the Classroom: How Many Are Here Today? (p. 82), describes one kindergarten teacher's experience with this activity and focuses on the variety of strategies students used to solve the problem. A second **Teacher Note,** Understanding Students' Work (p. 84), further explores the approaches described in From the Classroom to help you analyze and assess kindergartners' work.

It is not uncommon for students of this age to create a model that involves some action—for example, building a tower of 25 cubes and taking away 4. Such an action might be difficult for students to represent. One option is to suggest that they dictate their problem-solving strategy to you. As students finish their models, suggest that they write a title (or dictate one). If there's enough space in the room, display the students' representations.

Observing the Students

As you watch students at work on their models, ask them about their ideas. Consider the following:

- Do students understand the problem? Are they able to explain it to another student? If not, restate the problem or ask another student to explain it. If students understand the problem but have difficulty thinking about how to represent the information in order to solve it, ask them to explain their idea and then help them select materials to use.
- What materials do students select and how do they use them?
- Do students use the total number of people in the class to help them solve the problem?
- Do students use counting strategies (such as comparing quantities, counting on, or counting back) to help solve the problem?
- How do students count and keep track of the data?
- Are students able to explain their strategy for solving the problem? Is their strategy apparent from their representation?

Gather the students where they can see one another's work.

You've found many different ways to show information about how many people are here today. Some of you used cubes, some used counters, and some used pictures.

Ask a few volunteers to explain their representations to the group. In order to show the range of possibilities, call on students who used different materials to represent the data. As each student shares, ask others to raise their hand if they used the same material for their representation. This will acknowledge each student's work without taking the time for everyone to share individually.

How We Solved the Problem

Focus Time Follow-Up

Counting Strategies Occasionally when you collect attendance data, choose one of the strategies that students used in this Focus Time to determine the number of people present. For example, pass out a button to each student, then collect the buttons and count them, or build a tower of cubes for the total number in the class and take one away for each absent student. Double-check the result by counting the people present.

Extension

Two Choices To follow this problem-solving activity, you may want students to do more Yes/No Surveys (p. 66) or to continue their work in The Grocery Store (p. 48). You might also include any other Choice Time activities from the unit or their variations.

Choice Time

Yes/No Surveys

The Grocery Store

Teacher Note

How Many Are Here Today?

I chose to present this activity to my students on a day when six students were absent. My kindergartners had been working in this data unit for about three weeks. They had done all the Focus Time and the Choice Time activities. The attendance problem I posed was somewhat familiar, in that every day during our morning class meeting we discussed whose names we should place on the absent list that was submitted to the school office. The number of students in the classroom was firmly established—24 was an important number to these students. On this day, we quickly determined that six students were absent. But what really surprised me was the range of responses to my question, "How many people do you think are here today?" The students' answers ranged from 10 to 22. I was also surprised by some students' apparent lack of number sense when it came to thinking about the numbers 24 and 6.

Most of my students were immediately interested in "proving" how many students were present today. They chose from materials that I had set out on a table, and most settled into making a representation of their strategy. Although I usually have students work on math problems during our morning Choice Time period, I decided to rearrange our schedule that day to allow time for everyone to work on the same problem. I was most interested in observing the ideas that the children had for solving a somewhat complicated problem.

Kelsey's idea was to make a tower of 24 cubes. "This," she said, "is when all of us are in school." She then took off 6 cubes, explaining, "Because these are the people who are sick. So if I count all of *these* cubes [the larger tower], that will be the people who are here today. I counted them before and it was 18."

Joel decided to give every student in the class a button. He then collected and counted all the buttons. "If everyone here takes one button, then I can count the buttons and that will tell me how many people are in school because one button, one person!"

Marisa made a chart with 24 stick figures to represent the 24 kids in our class. She then circled 6 of these figures and wrote "NT HER" (not here). She explained that if she counted the rest of the stick figures, that would be the number of students in school today.

Akeem wrote out the numbers from 1 to 24 to show the kids in the class. Then he crossed off six numbers: 24, 23, 22, 21, 20, 19. "This number here," he said, pointing to 18, "is who is left at school. I can count the numbers or I see that the last number not crossed off is 18, so that's how many people are in school."

Continued on next page

Shanae's process was similar to Kelsey's, although she used keys from our counting box rather than cubes to represent the people in our class. What I noted about Shanae's strategy was her explanation during the sharing meeting, which uncovered some difficulties in counting that I had not noticed before. As she was demonstrating to her classmates that she used 24 keys to show the 24 students in the class, she counted the keys inaccurately three times—each time losing track of the count at around 16. Eventually, with the help of a classmate, Shanae successfully counted the 24 keys.

What interested me was that Shanae's explanation clearly suggested that she had understood the problem and her strategy for solving it. Until she shared her work, I had not seen her difficulty with counting a set of objects. I questioned whether she was able to hold onto larger amounts and whether the bulkiness of the keys as counters made the counting task more difficult. I made a note to spend some time with Shanae during Choice Time.

Ruben was the only child who added to the number of people absent as a way of figuring out the number of people present. He first built a tower of six red cubes and then snapped together a long tower of blue cubes. "These," he said, "are the people here today because blue is my favorite color. I'll count them until I get to 24. See, 1, 2, 3, 4, . . . " He counted the red cubes to 6 first, and then counted on, using the blue cubes, all the way from 7 to 24.

My question to Ruben was, "So how many people are here today?"

"This many," he replied, holding up the tower of blue cubes.

When I asked, "How many is that?" he shrugged his shoulders. "Is there a way you could figure that out?" I asked.

Ruben said he could count them, and he did so, beginning with 1, touching each blue cube as he said the next number, arriving at 18. "There are 18 blues," he announced.

"So what does that tell you?" I asked.

"Um, how many people are here today?" Ruben still didn't seem entirely sure of what he had just counted.

Many students in the classroom chose to solve the problem using a strategy similar to Kelsey's and Shanae's, but counting out 24 objects to represent the total number of people was challenging. All could accurately take away six objects from the group, but their results varied because they didn't all start out with 24.

During sharing, a few students recognized that they had used similar strategies but arrived at different answers. Some of them were eager to change their representations, while others did not seem to care. In thinking more about this, I decided that the strength of this activity was giving these 5- and 6-year-olds an opportunity to solve a real-world problem based on data that were familiar and meaningful to them. Since talking about the attendance was one of our daily classroom routines, I planned to present this problem to students again and see how their strategies evolved.

The students described by the teacher in From the Classroom: How Many Are Here Today? (p. 82) represent different levels of understanding the problem and a range of problem-solving strategies. The samples of the students' work and descriptions of their sharing provide valuable insights into how kindergarten students think about this problem.

Kelsey saw this as a subtraction problem. She built a tower of 24 cubes and took away 6 cubes for the absent students. While a number of students used or attempted to use a strategy similar to Kelsey's, not all had as clear an understanding of what each group or number represented, and not all were successful in counting out 24 cubes.

Marisa's strategy of drawing 24 stick figures and circling the figures of the absent people is similar to the model that Kelsey used. For some young students, stick figures are easier to understand than cubes or other objects because they more closely resemble people. Marisa's solution suggests that she understands the problem and how to solve it.

Marisa's work

When Joel passed out one button to each student, then collected the buttons and counted them, he was using the idea of one-to-one correspondence to solve the problem. He was confident that the number of buttons represented the number of people present. He was able to use a model that represented the people without having to count the actual people. The information about the number of people absent was irrelevant with this strategy.

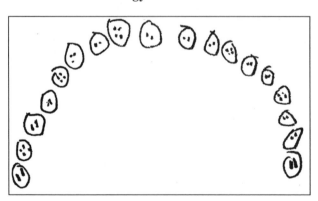

Joel's work. The buttons in a semicircle represent students sitting in the meeting area.

Akeem's work

Counting back, as Akeem did, is a method of subtraction. This method often poses problems for students because they do not have a clear sense of what the numbers represent. For example, counting back 6 from 24, they might say, "24, 23, 22, 21, 20, 19." They are then unsure which number—19 or the next lower number, 18—represents how many are left. Akeem's method of writing the numbers 1 to 24 and then crossing numbers out as he counted back gave him a concrete way of keeping track. In addition, it provided a visual picture of the count.

Ruben viewed the task as an addition problem, starting with six red cubes (the number of people absent) and adding on blue cubes until he arrived at the number of people in the whole class. While he represented the data accurately with cubes, he did not seem confident about what the parts of his model represented, so he had difficulty answering the question "How many people are in school today?" Had the teacher not observed Ruben and asked him to explain his model, this confusion might not have been apparent. Understanding parts and wholes and their relationships is an important idea throughout mathematics and one that students will encounter over and over again.

Shanae's strategy—counting out keys for her 24 classmates and removing six keys for the absent ones—was similar to Kelsey's in that both girls represented and solved the problem as a subtraction problem. The more important aspect of Shanae's work is the trouble she had counting and keeping track of what she was counting. Some kindergarten students are able to count by rote into the teens and above, but many have difficulty keeping track of that many objects. The teacher's reflective questions—whether the student was able to keep track of larger amounts and whether the bulkiness of the keys made the counting task more difficult—are important ones.

These examples suggest a range of responses to this attendance question, responses that you are likely to see in any kindergarten classroom. If you offer repeated experience in solving similar problems taken from real-world contexts, you will see students gradually expand and refine their strategies and ideas.

Choice Time is an opportunity for students to work on a variety of activities that focus on similar mathematical content. In the kindergarten *Investigations* curriculum, Choice Time is a regular feature that follows each whole-group Focus Time. The activities in Choice Time are not sequential; as students move among them, they continually revisit the important concepts and ideas they are learning in that unit. Many Choice Time activities are designed with the intent that students will work on them more than once. As they play a game a second or third time, use a material over and over again, or solve many similar problems, students are able to refine their strategies, see a variety of approaches, and bring new knowledge to familiar experiences.

Scheduling Choice Time

Scheduling of the suggested Choice Time activities will depend on the structure of your classroom day. Many kindergarten teachers already have some type of "activity time" built into their daily schedule, and the Choice Time activities described in each investigation can easily be presented during these times. Some classrooms have a designated math time once a day or at least three or four times a week. In these cases you might spend one or two math times on a Focus Time activity, followed by five to seven days of Choice Time during math, with students choosing among three or four activities. New activities can be added every few days.

Setting Up the Choices

Many kindergarten teachers set up the Choice Time activities at centers or stations around the room. At each center, students will find the materials needed to complete the activity. Other teachers prefer to keep materials stored in a central location; students then take the materials they need to a designated workplace. In either case, materials should be readily accessible. When choosing an arrangement, you may need to experiment with a few different structures before finding the setup that works best for you and your students.

We suggest that you limit the number of students doing a Choice Time activity at any one time. In many cases, the quantity of materials available establishes the limit. Even if this is not the case, limiting the number is advisable because it gives students the opportunity to work in smaller groups. It also gives them a chance to do some choices more than once.

In the quantity of materials specified for each Choice Time activity, "per pair" refers to the number of students who will be doing that activity at the same time (usually not the entire class). You can plan the actual quantity needed for your class once you decide how many other activities will be available at the same time.

Many kindergarten teachers use some form of chart or Choice Board that tells which activities are available and for how many students. This organizer can be as simple as a list of the activities on chart paper, each activity identified with a little sketch. Ideas for pictures to help identify each different activity are found with the blackline masters for each kindergarten unit.

In some classrooms, teachers make permanent Choice Boards by attaching small hooks or Velcro strips onto a large board or heavy cardboard. The choices are written on individual strips and hung on the board. Next to each choice are additional hooks or Velcro pieces that indicate the number of students who can be working at that activity. Students each have a small name tag that they are responsible for moving around the Choice Board as they proceed from activity to activity.

Introducing New Choices

Choice Time activities are suggested at the end of each Focus Time. Plan to introduce these gradually, over a few days, rather than all at once on the same day. Often two or three of the choices will be familiar to students already, either because they are a direct extension of the Focus Time activity or because they are continuing from a previous investigation. On the first day of

Choice Time, you might begin with the familiar activities and perhaps introduce one new activity. On subsequent days, one or two new activities can be introduced to students as you get them started on their Choice Time work. Most teachers find it both more efficient and more effective to introduce activities to the whole class at once.

Managing Choice Time

During the first weeks of Choice Time, you will need to take an active role in helping students learn the routine, your expectations, and how to plan what they do. We do not recommend organizing students into groups and circulating the groups every 15–20 minutes. For some students, this set time may be too long to spend at an activity; others may have only begun to explore the activity when it's time to move on. Instead, we recommend that you support students in making their own decisions about the activities they do. Making choices, planning their time, and taking responsibility for their own learning are important aspects of the school experience. If some students return to the same activity over and over again without trying other choices, sug-

gest that they make a different first choice and then do the favorite activity as a second choice.

When a new choice is introduced, many students want to do it first. Initially you will need to give lots of reassurance that every student will have the chance to try each choice.

As students become more familiar with the Choice Time routine and the classroom structure, they will come to trust that activities are available for many days at a time.

For some activities, students will have a "product" to save or share. Some teachers provide folders where students can keep their work for each unit. Other teachers collect students' work in a central spot, then file it in individual student folders. In kindergarten, many of the products will not be on tidy sheets of paper. Instead, students will be making constructions out of pattern blocks and interlocking cubes, drawing graphs on large pieces of drawing paper, and creating patterns on long strips of paper.

Continued on next page

For some activities, such as the counting games they play again and again, there may be no actual "product." For this reason, some teachers take photographs or jot down short anecdotal observations to record the work of their kindergartners.

During the second half of the year, or when students seem very comfortable with Choice Time, you might consider asking them to keep track of the choices they have completed. This can be set up in one of these ways:

- Students each have a blank sheet of paper. When they have completed an activity, they record its name or picture on the paper.

- Post a sheet of lined paper at each station, or a sheet for each choice at the front of the room. At the top of the sheet, write the name of one activity with the corresponding picture. When students have completed an activity, they print their name on the appropriate sheet.

Some teachers keep a date stamp at each station or at the front of the room, making it easy for students to record the date as well. As they complete each choice, students place in a designated spot any work they have done during that activity.

In addition to learning about how to make choices and how to work productively on their own, students should be expected to take responsibility for cleaning up and returning materials to their appropriate storage locations. This requires a certain amount of organization on the part of the teacher—making sure storage bins are clearly labeled, and offering some instruction about how to clean up and how to care for the various materials. Giving students a "5 minutes until cleanup" warning before the end of any Choice Time session allows students to finish what they are working on and prepare for the upcoming transition.

At the end of a Choice Time, spend a few minutes discussing with students what went smoothly, what sorts of issues arose and how they were resolved, and what students enjoyed or found difficult. Encourage students to be involved in the process of finding solutions to problems that come up in the classroom. In doing so, they take some responsibility for their own behavior and become involved with establishing classroom policies.

Observing and Working with Students

During the initial weeks of Choice Time, much of your time will be spent in classroom management, circulating around the room, helping students get settled into activities, and monitoring the process of making choices and moving from one activity to another. Once routines are familiar and well established, however, students will become more independent and responsible for their own work. At this point, you will have time to observe and listen to students while they work. You might plan to meet with individual students, pairs, or small groups that need help; you might focus on students you haven't had a chance to observe before; or you might do individual assessments. The section About Assessment (p. I-8) explains the importance of this type of observation in the kindergarten curriculum and offers some suggestions for recording and using your observations.

Materials as Tools for Learning

Concrete materials are used throughout the *Investigations* curriculum as tools for learning. Students of all ages benefit from being able to use materials to model problems and explain their thinking.

The more available materials are, the more likely students are to use them. Having materials available means that they are readily accessible and that students are allowed to make decisions about which tools to use and when to use them. In much the same way that you choose the best tool to use for certain projects or tasks, students also should be encouraged to think about which material best meets their needs. To store manipulatives where they are easily accessible to the class, many teachers use plastic tubs or shoe boxes arranged on a bookshelf or along a windowsill. This storage can hold pattern blocks, Geoblocks, interlocking cubes, square tiles, counters such as buttons or bread tabs, and paper for student use.

It is important to encourage all students to use materials. If manipulatives are used only when someone is having difficulty, students can get the mistaken idea that using materials is a less sophisticated and less valued way of solving a problem. Encourage students to talk about how they used certain materials. They should see how different people, including the teacher, use a variety of materials in solving the same problem.

Introducing a New Material: Free Exploration
Students need time to explore a new material before using it in structured activities. By freely exploring a material, students will discover many of its important characteristics and will have some understanding of when it might make sense to use it. Although some free exploration should be done during regular math time, many teachers make materials available to students during free times or before or after school. Each new material may present particular issues that

you will want to discuss with your students. For example, to head off the natural tendency of some children to make guns with the interlocking cubes, you might establish a rule of "no weapons in the classroom." Some students like to build very tall structures with the Geoblocks. You may want to specify certain places where tall structures can be made—for example, on the floor in a particular corner—so that when they come crashing down, they are contained in that area.

Establishing Routines for Using Materials
Establish clear expectations about how materials will be used and cared for. Consider asking the students to suggest rules for how materials should and should not be used; they are often more attentive to rules and policies that they have helped create.

Initially you may need to place buckets of materials close to students as they work. Gradually, students should be expected to decide what they need and get materials on their own.

Plan a cleanup routine at the end of each class. Making an announcement a few minutes before the end of a work period helps prepare students for the transition that is about to occur. You can then give students several minutes to return materials to their containers and double-check the floor for any stray materials. Most teachers find that establishing routines for using and caring for materials at the beginning of the year is well worth the time and effort.

Encouraging Students to Think, Reason, and Share Ideas

Students need to take an active role in mathematics class. They must do more than get correct answers; they must think critically about their ideas, give reasons for their answers, and communicate their ideas to others. Reflecting on one's thinking and learning is a challenge for all learners, but even the youngest students can begin to engage in this important aspect of mathematics learning.

Teachers can help students develop their thinking and reasoning. By asking "How did you find your answer?" or "How do you know?" you encourage students to explain their thinking. If these questions evoke answers such as "I just knew it" or no response at all, you might reflect back something you observed as they were working, such as "I noticed that you made two towers of cubes when you were solving this problem." This gives students a concrete example they can use in thinking about and explaining how they found their solutions.

You can also encourage students to record their ideas by building concrete models, drawing pictures, or starting to print numbers and words. Just as we encourage students to draw pictures that tell stories before they are fluent readers and writers, we should help them see that their mathematical ideas can be recorded on paper. When students are called on to share this work with the class, they learn that their mathematical thinking is valued and they develop confidence in their ideas. Because communicating about ideas is central to learning mathematics, it is important to establish the expectation that students will describe their work and their thinking, even in kindergarten.

There is a delicate balance between the value of having students share their thinking and the ability of 5- and 6-year-olds to sit and listen for extended periods of time. In kindergarten classrooms where we observed the best discussions, talking about mathematical ideas and sharing work from a math activity were as much a part of the classroom culture as sitting together to listen to a story, to talk about a new activity, or to anticipate an upcoming event.

Early in the school year, whole-class discussions are best kept short and focused. For example, after exploring pattern blocks, students might simply share experiences with the new material in a discussion structured almost as list-making:

What did you notice about pattern blocks? Who can tell us something different?

With questions like these, lots of students can participate without one student taking a lot of time.

Later in the year, when students are sharing their strategies for solving problems, you can use questions that allow many students to participate at once by raising their hands. For example:

Luke just shared that he solved the problem by counting out one cube for every person in our classroom. Who else solved the problem the same way Luke did?

In this way, you acknowledge the work of many students without everyone sharing individually.

Sometimes all students should have a chance to share their math work. You might set up a special "sharing shelf" or display area to set out or post student work. By gathering the class around the shelf or display, you can easily discuss the work of every student.

The ability to reflect on one's own thinking and to consider the ideas of others evolves over time, but even young students can begin to understand that an important part of doing mathematics is being able to explain your ideas and give reasons for your answers. In the process, they see that there can be many ways of finding solutions to the same problem. Over the year, your students will become more comfortable thinking about their solution methods, explaining them to others, and listening to their classmates explain theirs.

Games: The Importance of Playing More Than Once

Games are used throughout the *Investigations* curriculum as a vehicle for engaging students in important mathematical ideas. The game format is one that most students enjoy, so the potential for repeated experiences with a concept or skill is great. Because most games involve at least one other player, students are likely to learn strategies from each other whether they are playing cooperatively or competitively.

The more times students play a mathematical game, the more opportunities they have to practice important skills and to think and reason mathematically. The first time or two that students play, they focus on learning the rules. Once they have mastered the rules, their real work with the mathematical content begins.

For example, when students play the card game Compare, they practice counting and comparing two quantities up to 10. As they continue to play over days and weeks, they become familiar with the numerals to 10 and the quantities they represent. Later in the year, they build on this knowledge as they play Double Compare, a similar game in which they add and compare quantities up to 12. For many students, repeated experience with these two games leads them quite naturally to reasoning about numbers and number combinations, and to exploring relationships among number combinations.

Similarly, a number of games in *Pattern Trains and Hopscotch Paths* build and reinforce students' experience with repeating patterns. As students play Make a Train, Break the Train, and Add On, they construct and extend a variety of repeating patterns and are led to consider the idea that these linear patterns are constructed of units that repeat over and over again.

Games in the geometry unit *Making Shapes and Building Blocks,* such as Geoblock Match-Up, Build a Block, and Fill the Hexagons, expose students again and again to the structure of shapes and ways that shapes can be combined to make other shapes.

Students need many opportunities to play mathematical games, not just during math time, but other times as well: in the early morning as students arrive, during indoor recess, or as choices when other work is finished. Games played as homework can be a wonderful way of communicating with parents. Do not feel limited to those times when games are specifically suggested as homework in the curriculum; some teachers send home games even more frequently. One teacher made up "game packs" for loan, placing directions and needed materials in resealable plastic bags, and used these as homework assignments throughout the year. Students often checked out game packs to take home, even on days when homework was not assigned.

Attendance

Taking the daily attendance and talking about who is and who is not in school are familiar activities in many kindergarten classrooms. Through the Attendance routine, students get repeated practice in counting a quantity that is significant to them: the number of people in their class. This is real data that they see, work with, and relate to every day. As they count the boys and girls in their class or the cubes in the attendance stick, they are counting quantities into the 20s. They begin to see the need to develop strategies for counting, including ways to double-check and to organize or keep track of a count.

Counting is an important mathematical idea in the kindergarten curriculum. As students count, they are learning how our number system is constructed, and they are building the knowledge they need to begin to solve numerical problems. They are also developing critical understandings about how numbers are related to each other and how the counting sequence is related to the quantities they are counting.

In *Investigations,* students are introduced to the Attendance routine during the first unit of the kindergarten sequence, *Mathematical Thinking in Kindergarten.* The basic activity is described here, followed by suggested variations for daily use throughout the school year.

The Attendance routine, with its many variations, is a powerful activity for 5- and 6-year-olds and one they never seem to tire of, perhaps because it deals with a topic that is of high interest: themselves and their classmates!

Materials and Preparation

The Attendance routine involves an attendance stick and name cards or "name pins" to be used with a display board. (Many teachers begin the year with name cards and later substitute name pins as a tool for recording the data.)

To make the attendance stick you need interlocking cubes of a single color, one for each class member, and dot stickers to number the cubes.

To make name cards, print each student's first name on a small card (about 2 by 3 inches). Add a photo if possible. If you don't have school photos or camera and film, you might ask students to bring in small photos of themselves from home.

For "name pins," print each student's name on both sides of a clothespin, being sure the name is right side up whether the clip is to the right or to the left.

Name cards might be displayed in two rows on the floor or on a display board. The board should have "Here" and "Not Here" sections, each divided into as many rows or columns as there are students in your class. To display name cards on the board, you might use pockets, cup hooks, or small pieces of Velcro or magnetic tape. Name pins can be clipped down the sides of a sturdy vertical board.

Collecting Attendance Data

How Many Are We? With the whole group, establish the total number of students in the class this year by going around the circle and counting the number of children present.

Encourage students to count aloud with you. The power of the group can often get the class as a whole much further in the counting sequence than many individuals could actually count. While one or two children may be able to count to the total number of students in the class, do not be surprised or concerned if, by the end of your count, you are the lone voice. Students learn the counting sequence and how to count by having many opportunities to count, and to see and hear others counting.

When you have counted those present, acknowledge any absent students and add them to the total number in your class.

Counting Around the Circle Counting Around the Circle is a way to count and double-check the number of students in a group. Designate one person in the circle as the first person and begin counting off. That is, the first person says "1," the second person says "2," and so on around the circle. As students are learning how to count around the circle, you can help by pointing to the person whose turn it is to count. Some students will likely need help with identifying the next number in the counting sequence. Encouraging students to help each other figure out what number might come next establishes a climate of asking for and giving help to others.

Counting Around the Circle takes some time for students to grasp—both the procedure itself and its meaning. For some students, it will not be apparent that the number they say stands for the number of people who have counted thus far. A common response from kindergartners first learning to count off is to relate the number they say to a very familiar number, their age. Expect someone to say, for example, "I'm not 8, I'm 5!" Be prepared to explain that the purpose of counting off is to find out how many students are in the circle, and that the number 8 stands for the people who have been counted so far.

Representing Attendance Data

The Attendance Stick An attendance stick is a concrete model, made from interlocking cubes, that represents the total number of students in the classroom. For young students, part of knowing that there are 25 students in the class is seeing a representation of 25 students. The purpose of this classroom routine is not only to familiarize students with the counting sequence of numbers above 10, but also to help students relate these numbers to the quantities that they represent.

To make an attendance stick, distribute an interlocking cube to each student in the class. After counting the number of students present, turn their attention to the cubes.

We just figured out that there are [25] students in our classroom today. When you came to group meeting this morning, I gave everybody

one cube. Suppose we collected all the cubes and snapped them together. How many cubes do you think we would have?

Collect each student's cube and snap them together into a vertical tower or stick. Encourage students to count with you as you add on cubes. Also add cubes for any absent students.

Ayesha is not here today. Right now our stick has 24 cubes in it because there are 24 students in school today. If we add Ayesha's cube, how many cubes will be in our stick?

Using small dot stickers, number the cubes. Display the attendance stick prominently in the group meeting area and refer to it each time you take attendance.

By counting around, we found that 22 of you are here today. Let's count up to 22 on the attendance stick. Count with me: 1, 2, 3 . . . *[when you reach 22, snap off the remaining cubes].* **So this is how many students are not here—who wants to count them?**

In this way, every day the class sees the attendance stick divided into two parts to represent the students HERE and NOT HERE.

Name Cards or Name Pins Name cards or pins are another concrete way to represent the students. Whereas the attendance stick represents *how many students* are in the class, name cards or pins provide additional data about *who* these people are.

Once students can recognize their name in print, they can simply select their card or pin from the class collection as they enter the classroom each day. At a group meeting, the names can be displayed to show who is here and who is not here, perhaps as a graph on the floor or on some type of display board.

Examining Attendance Data

Comparing Groups In addition to counting, the Attendance routine offers experience with part-whole relationships as students divide the total number into groups, such as PRESENT and ABSENT (HERE and NOT HERE) or GIRLS and BOYS. As they compare these groups, they are beginning to analyze the data and compare quantities: Which is more? Which is less? *How many* more or less? While the numbers for the groups can change on any given day, the sum of the two groups remains the same. Understanding part-whole relationships is a central part of both sound number sense and a facility with numbers.

The attendance stick and the name cards or name pins are useful tools for representing and comparing groups. One day you might use the attendance stick to count and compare how many students are present and absent; another day you might use name cards or pins the same way. Once students are familiar with the routine, you can represent the same data using more than one tool.

To compare groups, choose a day when everyone is in school. Count the number of boys and the number of girls.

Are there more boys than girls? How do you know? How many more?

Have the boys make a line and the girls make a line opposite them. Count the number of students in each line and compare the two lines.

Which has more? How many more?

Use the name cards or the attendance stick to double-check this information.

Once the total number of boys and girls is established, you can use this information to make daily comparisons.

Count the number of girls. Are all the girls HERE today? If not, how many are NOT HERE? How do you know? Can we show this information using the name cards? *[Repeat for the boys.]*

If we know that two girls and two boys are NOT HERE, how many in all are NOT HERE in school today? How do you know? Let's use the name cards to double-check.

When students are very familiar with this routine, with the total number in their class, and with making and comparing groups, you can

pose a more difficult problem. For example:

If we know four students are NOT HERE in school today, how many students are HERE today? What are all the ways we can figure that out, without counting off?

Some students might suggest breaking four cubes off the attendance stick and counting the rest. Others might suggest counting back from the total number of students. Still others might suggest counting up from 4 to the total number of students.

In addition to being real data that students can see and relate to every day, attendance offers manageable numbers to work with. Repetition of this routine over the school year is important; only after students are familiar with the routine will they begin to focus on the numbers involved. Gradually, they will start to make some important connections between counting and comparing quantities.

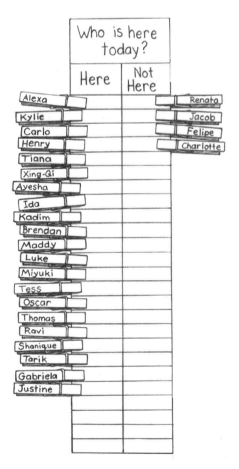

Counting Jar

Counting is the foundation for much of the number work that students do in kindergarten and in the primary grades. Children learn to count by counting and hearing others count. Similarly, they learn about quantity through repeated experiences with organizing and counting sets of objects. The Counting Jar routine offers practice with all of these.

When students count sets of objects in the jar, they are practicing the counting sequence. As in the Attendance routine, they begin to see the need to develop strategies for counting, including ways to double-check and keep track of what they have counted. By recording the number of objects they have counted, students gain experience in representing quantity and conveying mathematical information to others. Creating a new equivalent set gives them not only another opportunity to count, but also a chance to compare the two amounts.

Does my set have the same number as the set in the jar? How do I know?

The jar has 8 and I have 7. I need 1 more because 8 is 1 more than 7.

As students work, they are developing a real sense of both numbers and quantities.

The Counting Jar routine is introduced in the first unit of the kindergarten curriculum, *Mathematical Thinking in Kindergarten.* The basic activity is described here, followed by suggested variations for use throughout the school year on a weekly basis.

Materials and Preparation

Obtain a clear plastic container, at least 6 inches tall and 4–5 inches in diameter. Fill it with a number of interesting objects that are uniform in size and not too small, such as golf or table tennis balls, small blocks or tiles, plastic animals, or walnuts in the shell. The total should be a number that is manageable for most students in your class; initially, 5 to 12 objects would be appropriate quantities.

Prepare a recording sheet on chart paper. At the top, write *The Counting Jar,* followed by the name of the material inside. Along the bottom, write a number line. Some students might use this number line to help them count objects or as a reference for writing numerals. Place each number in a box to clearly distinguish one from another.

Laminate this chart so that students can record their counts on the chart with stick-on notes, write-on/wipe-off markers, or small scraps of paper and tape; these can later be removed and the chart reused.

Also make available one paper plate for each student and sets of countable materials, such as cubes, buttons, keys, teddy bear counters, or color tiles, so that students can create a new set of materials that corresponds to the quantity in the Counting Jar.

Counting

How Many in the Jar? This routine has three basic steps:

■ Working individually or in pairs, students count the objects in the Counting Jar.

■ Students make a representation that shows how many objects are in the jar and place their response on the chart.

■ Students count out another set of objects equivalent to the quantity in the Counting Jar. They place this new set on a paper plate, write their name on the plate, and display their equivalent collection near the Counting Jar.

As you use the Counting Jar throughout the school year, call attention to it in a whole-group meeting whenever you have changed the material or the amount inside the jar. Then leave it in a convenient location for two or three days so that everyone has a chance to count. After most students have counted individually, meet with the whole class and count the contents together.

Note: Some kindergarten teachers use a very similar activity for estimation practice. We exclude the task of estimation from the basic activity because until students have a sense of quantity, a sense of how much 6 is, a sense of what 10 balls look like compared to 10 cubes, it is difficult for them to estimate or predict how large a quantity is. When students are more familiar with the routine and have begun to develop a sense of quantity, you might include the variations suggested for estimation.

One More, One Less When students can count the materials in the jar with a certain amount of accuracy and understanding, try this variation for work with the ideas "one more than" and "one less than." As you offer the Counting Jar activity, ask students to create a set of objects with one more (or less) than the amount in the jar.

Filling the Jar Ourselves When the Counting Jar routine is firmly established, give individuals or pairs of students the responsibility for filling the jar. Discuss with them an appropriate quantity to put in the jar or suggest a target number, and let students decide on suitable objects to put in the jar.

At-Home Counting Jars Suggest to families that they set up a Counting Jar at home. Offer suggestions for different materials and appropriate quantities. Family members can take turns putting sets of objects in the jar for others to count.

Estimation

Is It More Than 5? To introduce the idea of estimation, show students a set of five objects identical to those in the Counting Jar. This gives students a concrete amount for reference to base their estimate on. As they look at the known quantity, ask them to think about whether there are *more than* five objects in the jar. The number in the reference group can grow as the number of objects in the jar changes, and you can begin to ask "Is the amount in the jar more than 8? more than 10?"

More or Less Than Yesterday? You can also encourage students to develop estimation skills when the material in the jar stays the same over several days but the quantity changes. In this situation, students can use reasoning like this:

Last time, when there were 8 blocks in the jar, it was filled up to *here*. Now it's a little higher, so I think there are 10 or 11 blocks.

Calendar

"Calendar," with its many rituals and routines, is a familiar kindergarten activity. Perhaps the most important idea, particularly for young students, is viewing the calendar as a real-world tool that we use to keep track of time and events. As students work with the calendar, they become more familiar with the sequence of days, weeks, and months, and relationships among these periods of time. Time and the passage of time are challenging ideas for most 5- and 6-year-olds, and the ideas need to be linked to their own direct experiences. For example, explaining that an event will occur *after* a child's birthday or *before* a familiar holiday will help place that event in time for them.

The Calendar routine is introduced in the first unit of the kindergarten curriculum, *Mathematical Thinking in Kindergarten*. The basic activity is described here, followed by suggested variations for daily use throughout the school year.

Materials and Preparation

In most kindergarten classrooms, a monthly calendar is displayed where everyone can see it when the class gathers as a whole group. A calendar with date cards that can be removed or rearranged allows for greater flexibility than one without. Teachers make different choices about how to display numbers on this calendar. We recommend displaying all the days, from 1 to 30 or 31, all month long. This way the sequence of numbers and the total number of days are

always visible, thus giving students a sense of the month as a whole.

You can use stick-on labels to highlight special days such as birthdays, class trips or events, non-school days, or holidays. Similarly, find some way to identify *today* on the calendar. Some teachers have a special star or symbol to clip on today's date card, or a special tag, much like a picture frame, that hangs over today's date.

A Sense of Time

The Monthly Calendar When first introducing the calendar, ask students what they notice. They are likely to mention a wide variety of things, including the colors they see on the calendar, pictures, numbers, words, how the calendar is arranged, and any special events they know are in that particular month. If no one brings it up, ask students what calendars are for and how we use them.

At the beginning of each month, involve students in organizing the dates and recording special events on the calendar. The following questions help them understand the calendar as a tool for keeping track of events in time:

If our trip to the zoo is on the 13th, on which day should we hang the picture of a lion?

Is our trip tomorrow? the next day? this week?

What day of the week will we go to the zoo?

How Much Longer? Many students eagerly anticipate upcoming events or special days. Ask students to figure out how much longer it is until something, or how many days have passed since something happened. For example:

How many more days is it until Alexa's birthday?

Today is November 4. How many more days is it until November 10?

How many days until the end of the month?

How many days have gone by since our parent breakfast?

Ask students to share their strategies for finding the number of days. Initially many students will count each subsequent day. Later some students may begin to find answers by using their growing knowledge of calendar structure and number relationships:

> I knew there were three more days in this row, and I added them to the three in the next row. That's six more days.

Calculating "how many more days" on the calendar is not an easy task. Quite likely students will not agree on what days to count. Consider the following three good answers, all different, to this teacher's question:

Today is October 4. Ida's birthday is on October 8. How many more days until her birthday?

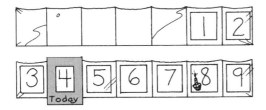

Tess: I think there are four more days because it's 4 . . . *[counting on her fingers]* 5, 6, 7, 8.

Ravi: There are three more days. See? *[He points to the three calendar dates between October 4 and October 8—5, 6, and 7—and counts three date cards.]*

Gabriela: It's five more days until her birthday. *[Using the calendar, she points to today and counts "1, 2, 3, 4, 5," ending on October 8.]*

All of these students made sense of their answers and, considering their reasoning, all three were correct. That's why, when asking "how many more?" questions based on the calendar, it is important also to ask students to explain their thinking.

Numbers on the Calendar

Counting Days The calendar is a place where students can daily visit and become more familiar with the sequence of counting numbers up to 31. Because the numbers on the calendar represent the number of days in a month, the calendar

is actually a way of *counting days.* You can help students with this idea:

Today is September 13. Thirteen days have already gone by in this month. If we start counting on 1, what number do you think we will end up on? Let's try it.

As you involve students in this way, they have another chance to see that numbers represent a quantity, in this case a number of days.

Missing Numbers or Mixed-Up Numbers Once students are familiar with the structure of the calendar and the sequence of numbers, you can play two games that involve removing and rearranging the dates. To play Missing Numbers, choose two or three dates on the monthly calendar and either remove or cover them. As students guess which numbers are missing, encourage them to explain their thinking and reasoning. Do they count from the number 1 or do they count on from another number? Do they know that 13 comes *after* 12 and *before* 14?

Mixed-Up Numbers is played by changing the position of numbers on the calendar so that some are out of order. Students then fix the calendar by pointing out which numbers are out of order.

Patterns on the Calendar

Looking for Patterns Some teachers like to point out patterns on the calendar. The repeating sequence of the days of the week and the months of the year are patterns that help students explore the cyclical nature of time. Many students quickly recognize the sequence of numbers 1 to 30 or 31, and some even recognize another important pattern on the calendar: that the columns increase by 7. However, in order to maintain the focus on the calendar as a tool for keeping track of time, we recommend using the Calendar routine only to note patterns that exist within the structure of the calendar and the sequence of days and numbers. The familiar activity of adding pictures or shapes to form repeating patterns can be better done in another routine, Patterns on the Pocket Chart.

Today's Question

Collecting, representing, and interpreting information are ongoing activities in our daily lives. In today's world, organizing and interpreting data are vital to understanding events and making decisions based on this understanding. Because young students are natural collectors of materials and information, working with data builds on their natural curiosity about the world and people.

Today's Question offers students regular opportunities to collect information, record it on a class chart, and then discuss what it means. While engaged in this data collection and analysis, students are also counting real, meaningful quantities (How many of us have a pet?) and comparing quantities that are significant to them (Are there more girls in our class or more boys?). When working with questions that have only two responses, students explore part-whole relationships as they consider the total number of answers from the class and how that amount is broken into two parts.

Today's Question is introduced in the first unit of the kindergarten curriculum, *Mathematical Thinking in Kindergarten.* The basic routine is described here, followed by variations. Plan to use this routine throughout the school year on a weekly basis, or whenever a suitable and interesting question arises in your classroom.

Materials and Preparation

Prepare a chart for collecting students' responses to Today's Question. If you plan to use this routine frequently, either laminate a chart so that students can respond with wipe-off markers, or set up a blank chart on 11-by-17-inch paper and make multiple photocopies. The drawback of a laminated wipe-off chart is that you cannot save the information collected; with multiple charts, you can look back at data you have collected earlier or compare data from previous questions.

Make a section across the top of the chart, large enough to write the words *Today's Question* followed by the actual question being asked.

Mark the rest of the chart into two equal columns (later, you may want three columns). Leave enough space at the top of each column for the response choices, including words and possibly a sketch as a visual reminder.

Leave the bottom section (the largest part of the chart) blank for students to write their names to indicate their response. Your chart will look something like this:

Later in the year, you may want a chart with write-on lines in the bottom section to help students to compare numbers of responses in the two or three categories. Be sure to allow one line for each child in the class. Lines are also helpful guides if you collect data with "name pins," or clothespins marked on both sides with student names, as suggested for the Attendance routine (see illustration on p. 95).

Choosing Questions

Especially during the first half of the school year, try to choose questions with only two responses. With two categories of data, students are more likely to see the part-whole relationship between the number of responses in each category and the total number of students in the class.

As your students become familiar with the routine and with analyzing the data they collect, you may decide to add a third response category. This is useful for questions that might not always elicit a clear yes-or-no response, such as these:

Do you think it will rain? *(yes, no, maybe)*

Do you want to play outside today? *(yes, no, I'm not sure)*

Do you eat lunch at school? *(yes, no, sometimes)*

As you choose questions and set up the charts for this routine, consider the full range of responses and modify or drop the question if there seem to be too many possible answers. Later in the year, as students become familiar with this routine, you may want to involve them in organizing and choosing Today's Question.

Questions About the Class With Today's Question, students can collect information about a group of people and learn more about their classmates. For example:

Are you a boy or a girl?

Are you 5 or 6 years old?

Do you have a younger brother?

Do you have a pet?

Did you bring your lunch to school today?

Do you go to an after-school program?

Do you like ice cream?

Did you walk or ride to school this morning?

Some teachers avoid questions about potentially sensitive issues (Have you lost a tooth? Can you tie your shoes?), while others use this routine to carefully raise some of these issues. Whichever you decide, it is best to avoid questions about material possessions (Does your family have a computer?).

Questions for Daily Decisions When you pose questions that involve students in making decisions about their classroom, they begin to see that they are collecting real data for a purpose. These data collection experiences underscore one of the main reasons for collecting data in the

real world: to help people make decisions. For example:

Which book would you like me to read at story time? (Display two books.)

Would you prefer apples or grapes for snack?

Should we play on the playground or walk to the park today?

Questions for Curriculum Planning Some teachers use this routine to gather information that helps them plan the direction of a new curriculum topic or lesson. For example, you can learn about students' previous experiences and better prepare them before reading a particular story, meeting a special visitor, or going on a field trip, with questions like these:

Have you ever read or heard this story?

Have you ever been to the science museum?

Have you ever heard of George Washington?

For questions of this type, you might want to add a third possible response (*I'm not sure* or *I don't know*).

Discussing the Data

Data collection does not end with the creation of a representation or graph to show everyone's responses. In fact, much of the real work in data analysis begins after the data has been organized and represented. Each time students respond to Today's Question, it is important to discuss the results. Consider the following questions to promote data analysis in classroom discussions:

What do you think this graph is about?

What do you notice about this graph?

What can you tell about [the favorite part of our lunch] by looking at this graph?

If we went to another classroom, collected this same information, and made a graph, do you think that graph would look the same as or different from ours?

Graphs and other visual representations of the data are vehicles for communication. Thinking about what a graph represents or what it is communicating is a part of data analysis that even the youngest students can and should be doing.

Patterns on the Pocket Chart

Mathematics is sometimes called "the science of patterns." We often use the language of mathematics to describe and predict numerical or geometrical regularities. When young students examine patterns, they look for relationships among the pattern elements and explore how that information can be used to predict what comes next. The classroom routine Patterns on the Pocket Chart offers students repeated opportunities to describe, copy, extend, create, and make predictions about repeating patterns. The use of a 10-by-10 pocket chart to investigate patterns of color and shape builds a foundation for the later grades, when this same pocket chart will display the numbers 1 to 100 and students will investigate patterns in the arrangement of numbers.

This routine is introduced in the second unit of the kindergarten curriculum, *Pattern Trains and Hopscotch Paths*. The basic routine is described here, followed by variations for use throughout the school year on a weekly basis.

Materials and Preparation

For this routine you will need a pocket chart, such as the vinyl Hundred Number Wall Chart (with transparent pockets and removable number cards). You will also need 2-inch squares of construction paper of different colors, a set of color tiles (ideally, the colors of the paper squares will match the tiles), and a set of 20–30 What Comes Next? cards. These cards, with a large question mark in the center, are cut slightly larger than 2 inches so they will cover the colored squares. A blackline master for these cards is provided in the unit *Pattern Trains and Hopscotch Paths*. You can easily make your own cards with tagboard and a marking pen.

For the variation Shapes, Shells, and Such, you can use math manipulatives such as pattern blocks and interlocking cubes, picture or shape cards, or collections of small objects, such as buttons, keys, or shells. The only limitation is the size of the pockets on your chart.

What Comes Next?

Before introducing this activity, arrange an a-b repeating pattern in the first row of the pocket chart using ten paper squares in two colors of your choice. Beginning with the fifth position, cover each colored square with a What Comes Next? (question mark) card.

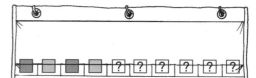

Gather students where the pocket chart is clearly visible and they have a place to work with color tiles, either on the floor or at tables.

Begin by asking students what they notice about the chart. Some may comment on the structure of the chart, some on the two-color pattern, and others may notice the question marks. Explain that each time they see one of these question marks, they should think "What comes next?" and decide what color might be under that card.

Provide each pair with a small cup of color tiles that match the paper squares. Ask students to build the first part of the pattern with color tiles and then predict what color comes next.

Who can predict, or guess, what color is hidden under each question mark on our chart? Use the tiles in your cup to show me what color would come next. How do you know?

Now, with your partner, see if you can make this pattern longer, using the tiles in your cup. Stop when your pattern has ten tiles.

When everyone has made a longer pattern, "read" the pattern together as a whole class. Verbalizing the pattern they are considering often helps students internalize it, recognize any errors in the pattern, and determine what comes next.

This basic activity can be done quickly, especially if students do not build the pattern with tiles. Many teachers integrate this routine into their group meeting time on a regular basis, making one or two patterns on the pocket chart and asking students to predict what comes next.

Initially, use only two colors or two variables in the patterns. In addition to a-b (for example, blue-green) repeating patterns, build two-color patterns such as a-a-b (blue-blue-green), a-b-b (blue-green-green), or a-a-b-b (blue-blue-green-green).

Variations

Making Longer Patterns When students are familiar with the basic activity, they can investigate what happens to an a-b pattern when it "wraps around" and continues to the next line. If the pattern continues in a left-to-right progression, the pattern that emerges is the same one older students see when they investigate the patterns of odd and even numbers on the 100 chart.

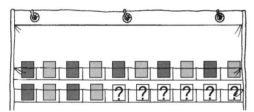

Shapes, Shells, and Such Color is just one variable for patterns; others can be made using a wide variety of materials and pictures.

shell, shell, button, shell, shell, button

triangle, square, triangle, square

Picture cards, sometimes used by kindergarten teachers to make patterns on the calendar, make great patterns on the pocket chart without the distraction of the calendar elements.

What Comes *Here*? Predicting what comes next is an important idea in learning about patterns. Also important is being able to look ahead and predict what comes *here?* even further down the line. Instead of asking for the *next* color in a pattern sequence, point to a pocket three or four squares along and ask students to predict the

color under that question mark. As you collect responses, ask students to explain how they predicted that color.

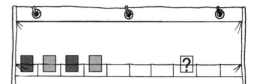

Border Patterns Explore a repeating pattern that extends around the entire outer edge of the pocket chart. Begin by filling the top row of the chart and asking what color would come next if this pattern turned the corner and went down the right side of the chart. Continue adding squares to finish the border. Every few days, begin a new pattern and ask students to help you complete the border. Start with a-b patterns. Gradually vary the pattern type, but continue to use only two colors, trying patterns such as a-a-b, a-b-b, a-a-b-b, or a-a-b-a. Ask students to notice which types make a continuous pattern all around the border and which do not.

With any border pattern, you can include a few What Comes Next? cards and ask students to predict the color of a particular pocket.

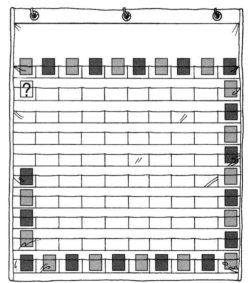

Patterns for Choice Time Hang the pocket chart where students can reach it. During free time or Choice Time, two or three students can work together to make their own pattern on the pocket chart, using colored paper squares or color tiles.

It is likely that more students with limited English proficiency will be enrolled in kindergarten than any other grade. Moreover, many will be at the earliest stages of language acquisition. By correctly identifying a student's current level of English, you can create appropriate stimuli to ensure successful communication when presenting activities from *Investigations*.

The four stages of language acquisition are characterized as follows:

- **Preproduction** Students do not speak the language at this stage; they are dependent upon modeling, visual aids, and context clues to obtain meaning.

- **Early production** Students begin to produce isolated words in response to comprehensible questions. Responses are usually yes, no, or other single-word answers.

- **Speech emergence** Students at this level now have a limited vocabulary and can respond in short phrases or sentences. Grammatical errors are common.

- **Intermediate fluency** Students can engage in conversation, producing full sentences.

You need to be aware of these four levels of proficiency while applying the following tips. The goal is always to ensure that students with limited English proficiency develop the same understandings as their English-speaking peers as they participate in this unit.

Tips for Small-Group Work Whenever possible, pair students with the same linguistic background and encourage them to complete the task in their native language. Students are more likely to have a successful exchange of ideas when they speak the same language. In other situations, teach all students how to make their communications comprehensible. For example, encourage students to point to objects they are discussing.

Tips for Whole-Class Activities To keep whole-group discussions comprehensible, draw simple sketches or diagrams on the board to illustrate key words; point to objects being discussed; use con-

trasting examples to help explain the attribute under discussion; model all directions; choose students to model activities or act out scenarios.

Tips for Observing the Students Assessment in the kindergarten units is based on your observations of students as they work, either independently or in groups. At times you will intervene by asking questions to help you evaluate a student's understanding. When questioning students, it is crucial not to misinterpret responses that are incomplete simply because of linguistic difficulties.

In many cases, students may understand the mathematical concept being asked about but not be able to articulate their thoughts in English. You need to formulate questions that allow students to respond at their stage of language acquisition in a way that indicates their mathematical understanding.

For example, the following question from Investigation 2, which focuses on students' ability to explain their thinking, is appropriate for students at the speech emergence and intermediate fluency stages of language acquisition: "Are students able to verbalize their ideas about like and unlike attributes [of two different shoes]?"

The question could be reworded as follows for students at the preproduction stage to elicit nonverbal responses: "Show me what is the same about these two shoes. Show me something that is different on each shoe."

For students at the early production stage, the following questions ask for one-word responses: "Are both shoes the same color? Are both shoes the same size? Are both shoes new?"

As you observe the students working, keep in mind which guidelines are appropriate for students at the different stages of language acquisition. Following is a categorization of typical questions from this unit.

Questions appropriate for students at the preproduction stage:

- How do students keep track of the items in their representations?
- Are students using an organizational system in their representations so that you can quickly see how many of each kind of block they grabbed?
- Are students able to sort the objects into two groups, one being a NOT group [not having a given attribute]?
- Are students able to sort the items in more than one way?

Questions appropriate for students at the early-production and early-speech-emergence stages:

- How do students count the number of chairs?
- How do students compare the number of chairs to the number of people in the class? Do they use counters? tallies? numbers? fingers?
- For each pair of objects, are students able to identify attributes that are the same and attributes that are different?
- How do students count and keep track of the data?

Questions appropriate for students at the late-speech-emergence and intermediate-fluency stages:

- Are students able to verbalize their ideas about like and unlike attributes?
- How do students describe the groups they have made? Can they explain their reasons for creating these groups?
- Do students discuss other ways of organizing the [class grocery] store besides putting identical foods together?
- Are students able to explain their survey results with such statements as "Most people in our class like carrots" or "More people have a pet than don't have a pet"?
- Were students able to choose a question that can be answered by only yes or no?

The following activities will help ensure that this unit is comprehensible to students who are acquiring English as a second language. The suggested approach is based on *The Natural Approach: Language Acquisition in the Classroom* by Stephen D. Krashen and Tracy D. Terrell (Alemany Press, 1983). The intent is for second-language learners to acquire new vocabulary in an active, meaningful context.

Note that *acquiring* a word is different from *learning* a word. Depending on their level of proficiency, students may be able to comprehend a word upon hearing it during an investigation, without being able to say it. Other students may be able to use the word orally, but not read or write it. The goal is to help students naturally acquire targeted vocabulary at their present level of proficiency.

body parts (nose, eyes, legs, etc.)

1. Ask students to stand up. Explain that they must follow your lead as you say and act out directions such as the following:

   Point to your nose.

   Blink your eyes.

   Shake one leg.

   Pat your head.

   Clap your hands.

   Touch your knees.

   Grab your elbows.

2. For variety, try changing the pace. Say and act out some commands in slow motion, others very fast, and others at normal speed.

clothing and color names

1. Cut small squares of construction paper in a wide range of colors.

2. Show the squares to students, then place them in a small box. Reach into the box and pull out one square, saying its color. Explain that when students see the card and hear the color, they should stand up quickly—if they are wearing something of that color.

3. After students have stood, point to and name the articles of clothing that match the color on the square.

   Xing-Qi is wearing a red shirt, the same color as this red paper.

4. Model one example and then play the game.

sort, group, same, different

1. Have ready about ten each of two different types of objects, such as cubes and teddy bear counters, mixed together. Place these together in a single pile.

2. Explain that you are going to *sort* these objects into two *groups* with the students' help. Start by sorting two or three of each object into two groups.

   This is the cube group *[point]*, **and this is the bear group** *[point]*.

3. Pick up another cube from the mixed group, and hold it next to the bear group.

   Is this the *same* as the bear counters?
   No, it's not the same; it's *different*.

   Hold the cube next to the cube group.

   Is this the same as the cubes?
   Yes, it's the same. This one goes in the cube group.

   Repeat with another one or two more objects.

4. Invite students to come up and sort the rest of the objects, one by one. For each item sorted, ask questions using the words *same* and *different*.

   Who would like to sort the next object?
   Is this object different from the others in the group? Is it the same?
   Are all the objects in this group the same now?

5. Repeat as needed with new objects to sort. Students might sort by color or size, using red and blue cubes, or small and large paper clips, for example. Each time, ask questions using the terms *same* and *different*.

typical lunch foods

1. On index cards, draw simple pictures of lunch foods favored by your students.

2. Display five of these pictures and identify each food by name.

3. Tell students to close their eyes while you remove one of the pictures.

4. Ask students to open their eyes, and explain that one picture is missing. Then ask questions to help them identify the missing picture.

   Is the [banana] *[point]* **still here?** (yes)
   Is the [sandwich] *[point]* **still here?** (yes)
   Is the [juice] *[point]* **still here?** (yes)
   What is missing—the [apple] or the [cookie]?

   Show the picture you removed to confirm the correct answer.

5. Repeat with another row of five pictures. Students can also be the ones to hide a picture.

Blackline Masters

Dear Family,

The new mathematics unit we are starting is called *Counting Ourselves and Others.* In this unit, the children will collect real information, or "data," by counting as they investigate questions like these: How many children are in our class—and how many eyes? How many chairs are there in our classroom? Is there a chair for every child? After the children have collected their data, they find ways to represent it to others. For example, they may draw pictures, or write numbers, or make a model with cubes or counters to show "how many."

Another part of our work in this unit involves sorting and classifying. The children look closely at related objects, such as two types of shoe. How are these shoes the same? How are they different? This information can be used to sort things into groups—for example, all the shoes with laces in one group, all the shoes without laces in another group. In other activities, they will be sorting and classifying containers, blocks of different colors and shapes, items of clothing, and their own self-portraits.

Throughout this unit your child will be collecting real data from classmates. In one activity, the children each identify their favorite part of lunch. Then they sort these favorite foods into categories and make a large class representation of this information. Later the children will be taking surveys in class, asking questions that can be answered yes or no, and finding ways to represent their results.

While we are working on this unit, you may want to be involved in one of these ways:

- Continue to count things around the house with your child. How many cans of soup are on the shelf? How many spoons are in the drawer? Ask your child to keep track of the counts and then find a way to communicate that information to someone else.

- Play "Same and Different." Find two similar objects, such as a sneaker and a boot, or a T-shirt and a shirt with buttons. With your child, take turns describing how the two things are the same and how they are different.

Thank you for your interest and participation in our mathematics activities.

Sincerely,

COUNTING EYES AT HOME

Dear Family,

In class, we have counted the number of eyes in our classroom.

At home, the children are going to collect information about the eyes of the people in their family.

Some children will draw pictures of this information. Others might use words, numbers, or a combination of words, numbers, and pictures.

You can help by listening to your child's plan for recording this information. Ask questions like these: "Is there a way you could show what color your sister's eyes are?" and "How can you make sure that you have included everyone in our family?"

Encourage your child to represent the information in whatever way makes sense to him or her.

HELP STOCK OUR CLASS STORE

Dear Family,

Some of the activities we will do in the next few weeks require common household objects. In one of the activities, we set up a classroom grocery store.

If you can lend us any of the following items, please send them to school with your child:

empty boxes (cereal boxes, cracker boxes, or other grocery items)

empty plastic bottles (with labels)

unopened cans (put your name on the bottom with masking tape, and we'll return them)

paper bags of different sizes

egg cartons

other empty grocery containers

Thanks for your help!

Same and Different

We compared _____

Same	Different

Yes/No Survey Chart

YES	NO

Choice Board art for
Self-Portraits

Choice Board art for
Counting Chairs

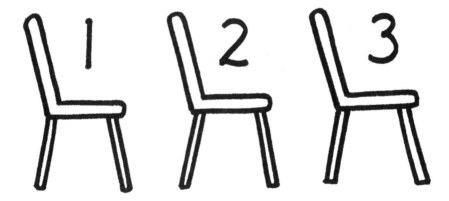

Choice Board art for
Pattern Block Grab

General Resource
Counting Ourselves and Others

Choice Board art for
Same and Different

Choice Board art for
Boxes, Bottles, and Cans

Choice Board art for
The Grocery Store

Choice Board art for
Clothing Sort

Choice Board art for
Yes/No Surveys

YES | NO